SACRED SCRIPTURE

WHITE HORSE

Sacred Scripture

White Horse

The Portable New Century Edition

EMANUEL SWEDENBORG

Translated from the Latin by George F. Dole
and Jonathan S. Rose

SWEDENBORG FOUNDATION
West Chester, Pennsylvania

Originally published in Latin as two separate works:

   Sacred Scripture: *Doctrina Novae Hierosolymae de Scriptura Sacra* (Amsterdam, 1763)
   White Horse: *De Equo Albo, de Quo in Apocalypsi, Cap. XIX: Et Dein de Verbo et Ejus Sensu Spirituali seu Interno, ex Arcanis Coelestibus* (London, 1758)

Second printing, with corrections, 2022

Printed in the United States of America

ISBN (Portable)   **978-0-87785-414-2**
ISBN (e-book of Portable Edition)   978-0-87785-679-5
The text of *Sacred Scripture* is also included in the hardcover library edition of *The Shorter Works of 1763*, ISBN 978-0-87785-503-3; and in the e-book form of that volume, ISBN 978-0-87785-707-5. The text of *White Horse* is also included in the hardcover library edition of *The Shorter Works of 1758*, ISBN 978-0-87785-482-1; and in the e-book form of that volume, ISBN 978-0-87785-700-6.

Library of Congress Cataloging-in-Publication Data

Swedenborg, Emanuel, 1688–1772.
   [Works. Selections]
   Sacred scripture ; White horse / Emanuel Swedenborg ; translated from the Latin by George F. Dole. — The portable new century edition.
      pages cm
   Includes bibliographical references.
   ISBN 978-0-87785-414-2 (pbk. : alk. paper) 1. New Jerusalem Church—Doctrines. 2. Bible. Revelation, XIX, 11–16—Commentaries. I. Swedenborg, Emanuel, 1688–1772. Doctrina Novae Hierosolymae de Scriptura Sacra. English. II. Swedenborg, Emanuel, 1688–1772. De equo albo, de quo in Apocalypsi, cap. XIX. English. III. Title. IV. Title: Sacred scripture. V. Title: White horse.
   BX8711.A7D6513 2015
   289'.4—dc23

                      2014042277

Senior copy editor, Alicia L. Dole
Text designed by Joanna V. Hill
Ornaments from the first Latin editions, 1763 and 1758
Typesetting by Alicia L. Dole and Mary M. Wachsmann
Cover designed by Karen Connor
Cover photograph by Magda Indigo

For information contact:
Swedenborg Foundation
320 North Church Street
West Chester, PA 19380 USA
Telephone: (610) 430-3222
Web: www.swedenborg.com
E-mail: info@swedenborg.com

Contents

v

White Horse

Conventions Used in This Work

*S*ACRED *Scripture* and *White Horse* are both small works on the meaning of the Bible, but they have not until now been paired with each other. *White Horse* was originally published in 1758 as a kind of topical index to Swedenborg's earlier and much larger work *Secrets of Heaven* (1749–1756). *Sacred Scripture* appeared in 1763 as the second of the so-called Four Doctrines (along with *The Lord, Life,* and *Faith*). As *Sacred Scripture* is the larger and more comprehensive of the two works, it appears before *White Horse* in this presentation. For introductory material on the content and history of *Sacred Scripture* and *White Horse,* and for annotations on their subject matter, with an extensive index, the reader is referred to the Deluxe New Century Edition volumes *The Shorter Works of 1758* and *The Shorter Works of 1763.* In general, the introductions in this series discuss the key ideas presented in each work, as well as the relationship of those ideas to the history of ideas, and specifically to their eighteenth-century context. The subsequent influence of the works is also treated. The annotations provide definitions of unfamiliar terms; clarification of direct or indirect references to people, places, events, or other works; and information on matters that present challenges to current readers because of changes in culture over time.

Section numbers Following a practice common in his time, Swedenborg divided his published theological works into sections numbered in sequence from beginning to end. His original section numbers have been preserved in this edition; they appear in boxes in the outside margins. Traditionally, these sections have been referred to as "numbers" and designated by the abbreviation "n." In this edition, however, the more common section symbol (§) is used to designate the section numbers, and the sections are referred to as such.

Subsection numbers Because many sections throughout Swedenborg's works are too long for precise cross-referencing, Swedenborgian scholar John Faulkner Potts (1838–1923) further divided them into subsections; these have since become standard, though minor variations occur from one edition to another. These subsections are indicated by bracketed numbers that appear in the text itself: [2], [3], and so on. Because the beginning of the first *subsection* always coincides with the beginning of the *section* proper, it is not labeled in the text.

SACRED SCRIPTURE | WHITE HORSE

Citations of Swedenborg's text As is common in Swedenborgian studies, text citations of Swedenborg's works refer not to page numbers but to section numbers, which unlike page numbers are uniform in most editions. In citations the section symbol (§) is generally omitted after the title of a work by Swedenborg. Thus "*Heaven and Hell* 239" would refer to section 239 (§239) of Swedenborg's *Heaven and Hell,* not to page 239 of any edition. Subsection numbers are given after a colon; a reference such as "239:2" indicates subsection 2 of section 239. The reference "239:1" would indicate the first subsection of section 239, though that subsection is not in fact labeled in the text. Where section numbers stand alone without titles, their function is indicated by the prefixed section symbol; for example, "§239:2".

Citations of the Bible Biblical citations in this edition follow the accepted standard: a semicolon is used between book references and between chapter references, and a comma between verse references. Therefore "Matthew 5:11, 12; 6:1; 10:41, 42; Luke 6:23, 35" refers to Matthew chapter 5, verses 11 and 12; Matthew chapter 6, verse 1; Matthew chapter 10, verses 41 and 42; and Luke chapter 6, verses 23 and 35. Swedenborg often incorporated the numbers of verses not actually represented in his text when listing verse numbers for a passage he quoted; these apparently constitute a kind of "see also" reference to other material he felt was relevant. This edition includes these extra verses and also follows Swedenborg where he cites contiguous verses individually (for example, John 14:8, 9, 10, 11), rather than as a range (John 14:8–11). Occasionally this edition supplies a full, conventional Bible reference where Swedenborg omits one after a quotation.

Quotations in Swedenborg's works Some features of the original Latin texts have been modernized in this edition. For example, Swedenborg's first editions generally rely on context or italics rather than on quotation marks to indicate passages taken from the Bible or from other works. The manner in which these conventions are used in the original suggests that Swedenborg did not feel it necessary to belabor the distinction between direct quotation and paraphrase; neither did he mark his omissions from or changes to material he quoted, a practice in which this edition generally follows him. One exception consists of those instances in which Swedenborg did not include a complete sentence at the beginning or end of a Bible quotation. The omission in such cases has been marked in this edition with added points of ellipsis.

Italicized terms Any words in indented scriptural extracts that are here set in italics reflect a similar emphasis in the first editions.

Swedenborg's footnote The author's footnote to *Sacred Scripture 6*, indicated by a superscript letter *a* in the main body of the text, consists of a cross-reference to one of his previously published works, *Heaven and Hell*.

Changes to and insertions in the text This translation is based on the first Latin editions, published by Swedenborg himself. It incorporates the silent emendation of minor errors, not only in the text proper but in Bible verse references and in section references to Swedenborg's other published theological works. The text has also been changed without notice where the verse numbering of the Latin Bible cited by Swedenborg differs from that of modern English Bibles. Throughout the translation, references or cross-references that were implied but not stated have been inserted in square brackets []; for example, [Matthew 22:40]. In contrast to such references in square brackets, references that occur in parentheses are those that appear in the first edition; for example, (John 3:27) and (as just noted). Occasionally square brackets signal an insertion of other material that was not present in the first edition. These insertions fall into two classes: words likely to have been deleted through a copying or typesetting error, and words supplied by the translator as necessary for the understanding of the English text, though they have no direct parallel in the Latin. The latter device has been used sparingly, however, even at the risk of some inconsistency in its application. Unfortunately, no annotations concerning these insertions can be supplied in this Portable edition.

Chapter numbering Swedenborg did not number the chapters of *Sacred Scripture* or *White Horse*. His decision not to do so seems to have been deliberate, and in accord with it chapter numbers are not included in the text. However, because some studies of his works make reference to chapter numbers, the table of contents provides them.

Biblical titles Swedenborg refers to the Hebrew Scriptures as the Old Testament and to the Greek Scriptures as the New Testament; his terminology has been adopted in this edition. As was the custom in his day, he refers to the Pentateuch (Genesis, Exodus, Leviticus, Numbers, and Deuteronomy) as the books of Moses, or simply as "Moses"; for example, in §44:2 he writes "This is what we read in Moses" and then cites a passage from Exodus. Similarly, in sentences or phrases introducing quotations he sometimes refers to the Psalms as "David." Conventional references supplied in parentheses after such quotations specify their sources more precisely.

Problematic content Occasionally Swedenborg makes statements that, although mild by the standards of eighteenth-century theological discourse, now read as harsh, dismissive, or insensitive. The most problematic are assertions about or criticisms of various religious traditions and their adherents—including Judaism, ancient or contemporary; Roman Catholicism; Islam; and the Protestantism in which Swedenborg himself grew up. These statements are far outweighed in size and importance by other passages in Swedenborg's works earnestly maintaining the value of every individual and of all religions. This wider context is discussed in the introductions and annotations of the Deluxe editions mentioned above. In the present format, however, problematic statements must be retained without comment. The other option—to omit them—would obscure some aspects of Swedenborg's presentation and in any case compromise its historicity.

Teachings
for the
New Jerusalem
on
Sacred Scripture

Teachings for the New Jerusalem
on Sacred Scripture

Sacred Scripture, or the Word,
Is Divine Truth Itself

E VERYONE *says* that the Word that comes from God is divinely **1**
inspired, and is therefore holy, but thus far no one knows where in
the Word this divine element is. This is because in the letter, the Word
seems pedestrian, stylistically strange, not sublime or brilliant the way
some literature of the present century is. That is why people who worship nature as God or who elevate nature over God and whose thinking therefore comes from themselves and their own interests rather than
from heaven and the Lord can so readily slip into error concerning the
Word and into contempt for it. When they read it they say to themselves,
"What's this? What's that? Is *this* divine? Can a God of infinite wisdom
say things like this? Where is its holiness, and where does its holiness
come from except people's religious bias and consequent credulity?"

People who think like this, though, are not taking into account the **2**
fact that Jehovah himself, who is the God of heaven and earth, spoke
the Word through Moses and the prophets, so the Word can be nothing but divine truth itself, because what Jehovah himself says is exactly

3

that. They are also not taking into account the fact that the Lord (who is the same as Jehovah) spoke the Word with the authors of the Gospels—much of it with his own mouth and the rest by means of the spirit of his mouth, which is the Holy Spirit. That is why he said that there was life in his words [John 6:63], that he was the light that enlightens [John 1:9], and that he was the truth [John 14:6]. [2] It is shown in *Teachings for the New Jerusalem on the Lord* 52–53 that Jehovah himself spoke the Word by means of the prophets.

See the Gospel of John for the fact that the words the Lord spoke with the authors of the Gospels are life:

> The words that I speak to you are spirit and are life. (John 6:63)

Again,

> Jesus said to the woman at Jacob's well, "If you knew the gift of God and who it is that is saying to you, 'Give me something to drink,' you would ask of him and he would give you living water. Those who drink of the water that I will give will not thirst to eternity; the water that I will give them will become a fountain of water within them, springing up into eternal life." (John 4:7, 10, 13, 14)

Jacob's well means the Word here, as it does also in Deuteronomy 33:28, so that is why the Lord sat there and spoke with the woman; and its water means the truth of the Word. [3] Again,

> Jesus said, "If any are thirsty, they must come to me and drink. As the Scripture says, from the bellies of those who believe in me will flow rivers of living water." (John 7:37, 38)

Again,

> Peter said to Jesus, "You have the words of eternal life." (John 6:68)

So in Mark the Lord says,

> Heaven and earth will pass away, but my words will not pass away. (Mark 13:31)

The reason the Lord's words are life is that he himself is life and truth, as he tells us in John:

> I am the way, the truth, and the life. (John 14:6)

And

> In the beginning was the Word, and the Word was with God, and the Word was God. In him there was life, and that life was the light for humankind. (John 1:1, 2, 3)

In this passage "the Word" means the Lord as divine truth, in which alone there is life and light.

[4] That is why the Word, which comes from the Lord and which is the Lord, is called "a fountain of living waters" (Jeremiah 2:13; 17:13; 31:9); "a fountain of salvation" (Isaiah 12:3); "a fountain" (Zechariah 13:1); and "a river of water of life" (Revelation 22:1). It is also why it says that "the Lamb who is in the midst of the throne will shepherd them and lead them to living fountains of waters" (Revelation 7:17).

There are passages as well where the Word is called a sanctuary and a tabernacle where the Lord dwells with us.

Earthly-minded people, though, are still not convinced by all this that **3** the Word is divine truth itself, containing both divine wisdom and divine life. They evaluate it by its style, where they do not see wisdom or life.

However, the style of the Word is the divine style itself, and no other style, however sublime and excellent it may appear to be, can be compared with it; that would be like comparing darkness to light.

It is characteristic of the Word's style that there is something holy in every statement, even in every word, even at times in the letters themselves; so the Word unites us to the Lord and opens heaven.

[2] There are two things that emanate from the Lord, divine love and divine wisdom, or (which amounts to the same thing) divine goodness and divine truth, since any divine goodness comes from his divine love, and any divine truth comes from his divine wisdom. In its essence, the Word is both, and since, as already stated, it unites us with the Lord and opens heaven, the Word fills us with good desires that come from love and truths that lead to wisdom, provided we read it with the help of the Lord and not just on our own. It fills our will with good desires that come from love and fills our understanding with truths that lead to wisdom. As a result, we gain life by means of the Word.

To free people from any doubt that this is the nature of the Word, **4** the Lord has revealed to me an inner meaning of the Word, a meaning that is essentially spiritual and that dwells within the outer meaning, which is earthly, the way a soul dwells within a body. This meaning is the spirit that gives life to the letter; therefore this meaning can bear witness to the divinity and holiness of the Word and be convincing even to earthly-minded people—if they are willing to be convinced.

There Is a Spiritual Meaning in the Word, Which Has Been Unknown until Now

THIS will be presented in the following sequence.

1. What the spiritual meaning is.
2. This spiritual meaning is throughout the Word and in all its details.
3. The spiritual meaning is what makes the Word divinely inspired and makes every word in it holy.
4. This meaning has not been recognized before.
5. From now on it can be given only to people who are focused on genuine truths that come from the Lord.

5 　1. *What the spiritual meaning is.* The spiritual meaning is not the meaning that shines forth from the Word's literal meaning when we study and interpret the Word in order to confirm some dogma of the church. That meaning is the literal meaning of the Word.

We cannot see the spiritual meaning in the literal meaning; it is within the literal meaning the same way the soul is within the body, thought is within the eyes, or a feeling is within a facial expression—the two act together as cause and effect.

It is primarily this meaning that makes the Word spiritual not only for us but for angels as well; so by means of this meaning the Word is in communication with the heavens.

6 　There emanate from the Lord what is *heavenly,* what is *spiritual,* and what is *earthly,* in that order. What emanates from his divine love is called *heavenly* and is divine goodness. What emanates from his divine wisdom is called *spiritual,* and is divine truth. What is *earthly* is a product of the two; it is a combining of them on the outermost level.

Angels of the Lord's heavenly kingdom, the ones who make up the third or highest heaven, are focused on the divine quality emanating from the Lord that is called heavenly, since they are focused on good desires that come from love, which they receive from the Lord. Angels of the Lord's spiritual kingdom, the ones who make up the second or middle heaven, are focused on the divine quality emanating from the Lord that is called spiritual, since they are focused on the truths that lead to wisdom, which they receive from the Lord.[a] We of the church in the world, though, are focused on a divine-earthly quality, which also emanates from the Lord.

[2] It follows from all this that as what is divine emanates from the Lord to its outermost limits, it comes down through three levels, and that they are called heavenly, spiritual, and earthly. The divine emanation that comes down to us from the Lord comes down through these three levels, and when it has come down it has these three levels within itself. Everything divine is like this, so when it is on its outermost level, it is full [of the inner levels].

That is what the Word is like.

In its outermost meaning it is earthly, in its inner meaning it is spiritual, and in its inmost meaning it is heavenly; and on every level of meaning it is divine.

It is not obvious from the literal meaning (which is earthly) that the Word is like this, because we here on earth have not known anything about the heavens before. This means that we have not known that spiritual quality or that heavenly quality; so we have not known the difference between them and what is earthly.

Then too, we cannot know what the difference between these qualities is unless we know about correspondence, since these three qualities are absolutely distinguishable from each other, like a goal, the means to it, and its result; or like the first, the intermediate, and the last. However, they coalesce by means of their correspondence, since what is earthly corresponds to what is spiritual and also to what is heavenly.

---

a. On the two kingdoms that make up the heavens, one called "the heavenly kingdom" and one called "the spiritual kingdom," see *Heaven and Hell* 20–28.

You may see what correspondence is, though, in *Heaven and Hell,* under the headings "The Correspondence of Everything in Heaven with Everything in the Human Being" (§§87–102) and "The Correspondence of Heaven with Everything Earthly" (§§103–115). There will be more to see in the examples from the Word cited below [§§9–17, 29, 35, 40–49, 79].

8   Since the Word is inwardly spiritual and heavenly, it was composed using nothing but correspondences; and when something is written by means of nothing but correspondences, its outermost written sense takes on the kind of style we find in the prophets and in the Gospels, a style that has divine wisdom and everything angelic hidden within it even though it seems to be commonplace.

9   2. *There is a spiritual meaning throughout the Word and in all its details.* There is no better way to make this clear than by using examples, such as the following. In the Book of Revelation, John says,

> I saw heaven opened, and behold, a white horse. And the one who sat on it was called faithful and true, and with justice he judges and makes war. His eyes were a flame of fire, and on his head were many gems. He had a name written that no one knew except him. He was clothed with a robe dipped in blood, and his name is called *the Word of God.* His armies in heaven, clothed in fine linen, white and clean, followed him on white horses. He has on his robe and on his thigh a name written: *King of Kings and Lord of Lords.* Then I saw an angel standing in the sun; and he cried with a loud voice, "Come and gather together for the great supper, so that you may eat the flesh of monarchs and the flesh of commanders, the flesh of the mighty, the flesh of horses and of those who ride on them, and the flesh of all people, free and slaves, both small and great." (Revelation 19:11–18)

No one can tell what this means except on the basis of the spiritual meaning of the Word; and no one can see the spiritual meaning except on the basis of a knowledge of correspondences, because all the expressions are correspondential, and there is not a word there that does not matter.

A knowledge of correspondences tells us the meaning of the white horse and of the one who sat on it, of the eyes that were like a flame of fire, of the gems that were on his head, of the robe dipped in blood, of the white linen worn by the people of his army in heaven, of the angel standing in the sun, of the great supper to which they were coming and gathering, also of the flesh of monarchs and commanders and the many others that they were to eat.

You may find what these particular expressions mean when spiritually understood in the booklet *White Horse* [§1], where these expressions are interpreted, so there is no need to give further interpretation here. That booklet shows that this is a description of the Lord as the Word, that his eyes like a flame of fire, the gems on his head, and the name written that no one knew except him mean the spiritual meaning of the Word and that no one knows it except him and those to whom he wills to reveal it [Matthew 11:27]; and the robe dipped in blood means the earthly meaning of the Word, its literal meaning, which has suffered violence. It is obvious that the Word is what is being described because it says "His name is called the Word of God"; and it is equally obvious that it means the Lord because it says that the name of the one who sat on the horse was written, "King of Kings and Lord of Lords."

The message that the spiritual meaning of the Word was to be opened at the close of the church is conveyed not only by what I have just said about the white horse and the one who sat on it but also by the great supper to which all were invited by the angel standing in the sun, so that they might come and eat the flesh of monarchs and commanders, of the mighty, of horses, of those who ride on them, and of all people, both free and slaves. All these expressions would be meaningless words, with neither life nor spirit, if there were nothing spiritual within them like a soul within a body.

In the twenty-first chapter of Revelation we find the following **10** description of the holy Jerusalem:

> Its light was like a most precious stone, like a jasper stone, clear as crystal. It had a great and high wall with twelve gates, and on the gates were twelve angels and the names written of the twelve tribes of the children of Israel. Its wall measured one hundred and forty-four cubits, which is the measure of a human being, that is, of an angel. The construction of its wall was of jasper, and its foundations were made of precious stones of every kind—jasper, sapphire, chalcedony, emerald, onyx, sardius, chrysolite, beryl, topaz, chrysoprase, jacinth, and amethyst. The twelve gates were twelve pearls. The city was pure gold, like clear glass, and was square—its length, breadth, and height were equal at twelve thousand stadia each. [Revelation 21:11–12, 16–21]

And so on.

We can tell that all these features are to be understood spiritually from the fact that the holy Jerusalem means a new church that the Lord is going to establish, as explained in §§62–65 of *Teachings on the Lord*. Further, since Jerusalem here means the church, it follows that everything said about it—about the city, its gates, its wall, the foundations of the wall, and its dimensions—has spiritual meaning in it, since what goes to make up the church is spiritual.

As for the meaning of the details, though, these have been explained in §1 of *The New Jerusalem and Its Heavenly Teachings* (published in London in 1758), so I forego further explanation.

Suffice it to say that we know from these examples that there is spiritual meaning in the details of the description of the city, like a soul within a body, and that if it were not for this meaning we would find nothing relevant to the church in what is written there—the city being of pure gold, the gates of pearls, the wall of jasper, the foundations of the wall of precious stones; the wall measuring a hundred and forty-four cubits by the measure of a human being, that is, of an angel; the city itself being twelve thousand stadia in length, breadth, and height; and so on.

Yet people who are familiar with the spiritual meaning because of their knowledge of correspondences understand that the wall and its foundations mean a body of teaching drawn from the literal meaning of the Word, and that the numbers twelve, a hundred and forty-four, and twelve thousand all mean much the same, namely, all the good and true features of the church viewed in one combined form.

11   It says in Revelation 7:[4–8] that one hundred and forty-four thousand were sealed, twelve thousand from each tribe of Israel: Judah, Reuben, Gad, Asher, Naphtali, Manasseh, Simeon, Levi, Issachar, Zebulun, Joseph, and Benjamin. The spiritual meaning of this is that everyone is saved who has accepted the church from the Lord. Being marked or sealed on the forehead, spiritually understood, means being recognized by the Lord and saved. The twelve tribes of Israel mean everyone from that church: twelve, twelve thousand, and one hundred and forty-four thousand mean all; Israel means the church; and each tribe means some particular aspect of the church. Anyone who does not know the spiritual content of these words may think that only that many people are going to be saved and that these will come only from the Israelite and Jewish people.

12   It says in chapter 6 of Revelation:

When the Lamb opened the first seal of the scroll a white horse came forth, and the one who sat on it had a bow and was given a crown. When he opened the second seal a red horse came forth, and the one who sat on it was given a great sword. When he opened the third seal a black horse came forth, and the one who sat on it had a pair of scales in his hand. When he opened the fourth seal a pale horse came forth, and the name of the one who sat on it was Death. [Revelation 6:1–8]

The only way to decipher this is by means of its spiritual meaning, and it is fully deciphered when we know the meaning of the opening of seals, a horse, and so on. These serve to describe successive states of the church from beginning to end with reference to its understanding of the Word.

The opening of the seals of the book by the Lamb means the Lord's bringing those states of the church out into the open.

A horse means the understanding of the Word.

The white horse means an understanding of the truth of the Word during the first state of the church.

The bow of the one who sat on the horse means the teachings about caring and faith that fight against false beliefs.

The crown means eternal life as the reward of victory.

[2] *The red horse* means the understanding of the Word during the second state of the church: in ruins with respect to what is good.

The great sword means false principles fighting against what is true.

The black horse means the understanding of the Word during the third state of the church: in ruins with respect to what is true.

The pair of scales means thinking truth has so little value that it is virtually worthless.

The pale horse means the absence of any understanding of the Word in the fourth or final state of the church, because of evil lives and consequent false beliefs.

Death means eternal damnation.

It is not obvious in the literal or earthly meaning that this is what is intended in the spiritual meaning; so unless that spiritual meaning is opened at last, the Word will remain closed in regard to this passage and the rest of the Book of Revelation—so tightly closed that no one will know where in that book anything holy or divine is hidden.

This is equally true of the meaning of the four horses and the four chariots coming out from between the two mountains of bronze in Zechariah 6:1–8.

In chapter 9 of Revelation we read,

13

The fifth angel sounded. And I saw a star fallen from heaven to the earth. To him was given the key to the bottomless pit. And he opened

the bottomless pit, and smoke arose out of the pit like the smoke of a
great furnace; and the sun and the air were darkened because of the
smoke of the pit. And out of the smoke locusts came onto the earth.
And to them was given power, as the scorpions of the earth have power.
The shapes of the locusts were like horses prepared for battle. On their
heads were what seemed to be golden crowns, and their faces were like
human faces. They had hair like women's hair, and their teeth were
like those of lions. They had breastplates of iron, and the sound of
their wings was like the sound of chariots with many horses running
into battle. And they had tails like scorpions, and there were stingers in
their tails. Their power was to hurt people for five months. And they
had as king over them the angel of the bottomless pit, whose name in
Hebrew is Abaddon, but in Greek he has the name Apollyon. [Revelation 9:1–3, 7–11]

Readers will not understand this either unless the spiritual meaning has
been unveiled to them, because nothing in it is an empty statement.
Everything, every detail, has meaning. It is about the state of the church
when all the truth it has recognized in the Word lies in ruins, and when
those who have become limited to their physical senses therefore convince themselves that falsities are truths.

[2] *The star fallen from heaven* means the ruined state of the truth
that was once recognized.

The darkened sun and air mean the light of truth turned into darkness.

The locusts that came out of the smoke of the pit mean false beliefs
built on the outward kind of thinking characteristic of people who have
become limited to their physical senses and see and evaluate everything
on the basis of deceptive appearances.

Scorpions mean the force of their rhetoric.

The locusts looking like horses prepared for battle means their rationalizing as though they understood what was true.

*The locusts having what seemed to be golden crowns on their heads and
having faces that looked human* means that it seemed to them that they
were triumphant and wise.

Their having hair like women's hair means that it seemed to them that
they were genuinely devoted to truth.

Their having teeth like those of lions means that their sensory impressions (which are the most superficial aspects of the earthly self) seemed
to them to have power over everything.

[3] *Their having breastplates like breastplates of iron* means the arguments from deceptive appearances that they use in order to fight and prevail.

The sound of their wings being like the sound of chariots with many horses running into battle means their rationalizations, based on supposedly true teachings from the Word, for which they feel compelled to fight.

Their having tails like scorpions means their persuasive ability.

Their having stingers in their tails means their skills in using this ability to deceive.

Their having power to hurt people for five months means that they induce a kind of stupor in people who are devoted to understanding what is true and perceiving what is good.

Their having as king over them the angel of the abyss whose name is Abaddon and Apollyon means that their false principles come from hell, where all the people are totally materialistic and in love with their own intelligence.

[4] This is the spiritual meaning of these words, none of which is obvious in the literal meaning. It is the same throughout the Book of Revelation.

Bear in mind that, when spiritually understood, everything is bound together in an ongoing connection, and every single word in the literal or earthly meaning contributes to its elegant construction. So if one little word were taken away, a connection would be broken and a link would be lost. To prevent this from happening, the command not to take away a word is appended to the end of this prophetic book (Revelation 22:19). It is the same with the prophetic books of the Old Testament: so that nothing would be lost, the Lord's divine providence arranged that their details were counted right down to the letters, which was done by the Masoretes.

When the Lord speaks to his disciples about the close of the age, **14** which is the last time of the church, at the end of his predictions about the sequence of changes of state he says,

> Immediately after the affliction of those days the sun will be darkened, the moon will not give its light, the stars will fall from heaven, and the powers of the heavens will be shaken. Then the sign of the Son of Humanity will appear in heaven, and then all the tribes of the earth will wail; and they will see the Son of Humanity coming in the clouds of heaven with power and great glory. And he will send out his angels

with a trumpet and a loud voice, and they will gather his chosen people from the four winds, from one end of the heavens to the other. (Matthew 24:29, 30, 31)

[2] Spiritually understood, this does not mean that the sun and moon will be darkened, that the stars will fall from heaven, and that a sign of the Lord will appear in heaven and he will be seen in the clouds accompanied by angels with trumpets. Rather, the particular words are here used to mean spiritual events that have to do with the church, spiritual events about its state at its end. The underlying reason is that in the spiritual meaning the sun that will be darkened is the Lord as an object of love; the moon that will not give its light is the Lord as an object of faith; the stars that will fall from heaven are the knowledge of what is good and what is true that will come to an end; the sign of the Son of Humanity in heaven is the manifestation of divine truth; the tribes of the earth that will wail are a complete lack of true belief and of good actions that come from love; the coming of the Son of Humanity in the clouds of heaven with power and glory is the Lord's presence in the Word, and a revelation—the clouds being the literal meaning of the Word and the glory being the spiritual meaning of the Word. The angels with a trumpet and a loud voice mean heaven as our source of divine truth; and the gathering of the chosen people from the four winds, from one end of the heavens to the other, means a new kind of church, specifically its love and faith.

[3] It is obvious from the prophets that this does not mean the darkening of the sun and the moon and the falling of the stars to earth, because things like this are said there about the state of the church when the Lord will come into the world. It says in Isaiah, for example:

Behold, the fierce day of Jehovah is coming, a day of blazing wrath. The stars of the heavens and their constellations will not shine their light. The sun will be darkened in its rising, and the moon will not make its light shine. I will execute judgment upon the world for its malice. (Isaiah 13:9–11; 24:23)

In Joel,

The day of Jehovah is coming, a day of darkness and gloom; the sun and the moon will be darkened and the stars will withhold their light. (Joel 2:1, 2, 10; 3:15)

In Ezekiel,

> I will cover the heavens and darken the stars. I will cover the sun with a cloud, and the moon will not give its light. I will darken all the bright lights and bring darkness upon the land. (Ezekiel 32:7, 8)

The day of Jehovah means the Coming of the Lord, which happened when there was no longer anything good or true left in the church, and there was no knowledge of the Lord.

To show that many passages in the prophetic books of the Word of the Old Testament are not understood if we lack their spiritual meaning, I should like to cite just a few. This from Isaiah, for example: **15**

> Then Jehovah will rouse up a whip against Assyria, like the blow against Midian on the rock Oreb; his staff will be stretched out over the sea, and he will lift it against the way of Egypt. And it will happen on that day that his burden will depart from your shoulder and his yoke from your neck. He will come against Aiath; he will cross over into Migron. He will command his weapons against Michmash; they will cross Mabara. Gibeah will be a place of lodging for us; Ramah will tremble with fear; Gibeah of Saul will flee. Wail with your voice, daughter of Gallim! Listen to Laishah, unfortunate Anathoth! Madmenah will wander; the inhabitants of Gebim will gather together. In Nob is it still a day for standing firm? The mountain of the daughter of Zion, the hill of Jerusalem, will move its hand. Jehovah will cut down the tangled places in the forest with iron, and Lebanon will fall by means of the Mighty One. (Isaiah 10:24–34)

All we find here are names from which we learn nothing without the aid of the spiritual meaning, in which all the names in the Word point to matters of heaven and the church. We gather from this meaning that this passage refers to the ruin of the whole church by information that corrupted every true teaching and supported every false teaching.

[2] In another passage from the same prophet,

> On that day the rivalry of Ephraim will wane and the enemies of Judah will be cut off. Ephraim will not compete with Judah, and Judah will not trouble Ephraim, but they will swoop down upon the shoulder of the Philistines toward the sea. Together they will plunder the children of the east. Edom and Moab will be [subject to] the stretching out of

their hand. Jehovah will curse the tongue of the sea of Egypt and will shake his hand over the river with the vehemence of his spirit; and he will strike it into seven streams, to make a pathway [that can be trodden] with sandals. Then there will be a highway for the rest of his people, the remnant from Assyria. (Isaiah 11:11, 13–16)

Here too, only those who know what these particular names mean will see anything divine, when in fact this is about the Lord's Coming and what will happen then, as is perfectly obvious from the first ten verses of the chapter. So without the aid of the spiritual meaning, who would see what these statements in this sequence mean, namely, that if people are caught up in false beliefs because of ignorance but have not let themselves be led astray by evil tendencies, they will find their way to the Lord, and that the church will then understand the Word, so that their false beliefs will no longer harm them?

[3] It is much the same in other passages where there are no names, as in Ezekiel:

Thus says the Lord Jehovih: "Son of Humanity, say to every winged bird and to every beast of the field, 'Gather and come. Gather yourselves from all around for my sacrifice, which I am sacrificing for you, a great sacrifice on the mountains of Israel, so that you may eat flesh and drink blood. You will eat the flesh of the mighty and drink the blood of the rulers of the earth. You will eat fat until you are full and drink blood until you are drunk, from my sacrifice, which I am sacrificing for you. At my table you will eat your fill of horses and chariots and the mighty and every man of war. This is how I will establish my glory among the nations.'" (Ezekiel 39:17–21)

If readers do not know from the spiritual sense the meaning of a sacrifice, of flesh and blood, of horses, chariots, the mighty, and men of war, all they can conclude is that they are going to eat and drink things like this. The spiritual meaning, though, tells us that eating flesh and drinking blood from a sacrifice that the Lord Jehovih offers on the mountains of Israel means taking divine goodness and divine truth into ourselves from the Word. This passage is about summoning everyone to the Lord's kingdom, specifically the Lord's establishment of a church among the nations. Can anyone fail to see that flesh does not mean flesh and that blood does not mean blood in this text? The same holds true for drinking blood until we are drunk and eating our fill of horses, chariots, the mighty, and every man of war.

There are passages like this in a thousand other places in the prophets.

Lacking a spiritual understanding, no one would know why the prophet **16** Jeremiah was commanded to buy a belt and put it around his waist, not to put it in water, and to hide it in a crevice in the rocks near the Euphrates (Jeremiah 13:1–7). No one would know why the prophet Isaiah was commanded to take the sackcloth off his waist and the sandals off his feet and to go naked and barefoot for three years (Isaiah 20:2, 3). No one would know why the prophet Ezekiel was commanded to take a razor to his head and his beard and then to divide the hair, burning a third of it in the middle of the city, striking a third with a sword, and scattering a third to the wind; also, to bind a few hairs in his hems, and eventually to throw a few into the midst of a fire (Ezekiel 5:1–4). The same prophet was commanded to lie on his left side for three hundred ninety days and on his right side for forty days and to make himself a cake out of wheat, barley, millet, and spelt and bake it over cow dung and eat it; and at another time to make a siege wall and a mound against [an image of] Jerusalem and besiege it (Ezekiel 4:1–15). No one would know why the prophet Hosea was twice commanded to take a whore as his wife (Hosea 1:2–9; 3:2, 3), and other things of the same sort.

Beyond that, without a spiritual understanding who would know the meaning of all the objects in the tabernacle—the ark, for example, the mercy seat, the angel guardians, the lampstand, the altar of incense, the showbread on the table, its veils and curtains? Without a spiritual understanding, who would know the meaning of Aaron's sacred garments—his tunic, robe, ephod, the Urim and Thummim, his turban, and so on? Without a spiritual understanding, who would know the meaning of all the commandments about burnt offerings, sacrifices, grain offerings, and drink offerings, about Sabbaths and festivals? The truth is that every bit of what was commanded meant something about the Lord, heaven, and the church.

You can see clearly in these few examples that there is a spiritual meaning throughout the Word and in its details.

We can tell from the Lord's parables, which have a spiritual mean- **17** ing in their very words, that when he was in the world he spoke in correspondences—that is, he was speaking in spiritual terms when he was naming earthly things. The parable of the ten young women may serve as an example. He said,

> The kingdom of the heavens is like ten young women who took their lamps and went out to meet a bridegroom. Five of them were prudent and five were foolish. The foolish women took their lamps but

brought no oil. The prudent women took oil in their lamps. When the bridegroom was delayed, they all became drowsy and fell asleep. In the middle of the night there was a shout: "Behold, the bridegroom is coming! Go out to meet him." At that, all the women woke up and trimmed their lamps. The foolish women said to the prudent ones, "Give us some of your oil, because our lamps are going out." The prudent women replied, "There might not be enough for us and for you. Go instead to the sellers and buy some for yourselves." But while they were away buying some, the bridegroom arrived, and the women who were prepared went in with him to the wedding, and the door was closed. Later the other women came along and said, "Lord, Lord, open up for us." But he answered and said, "I tell you truly, I do not know you." (Matthew 25:1–12)

[2] Only people who know that there is such a thing as a spiritual meaning and what it is like will see that there is a spiritual meaning, and therefore something holy and divine, in the details of this parable. Spiritually understood, the kingdom of God means heaven and the church; the bridegroom means the Lord, the wedding means the marriage of the Lord with heaven and the church brought about by good actions that come from love and faith; the young women mean the people of the church, ten meaning all of them and five meaning some of them; the lamps mean truths we believe; the oil means a love for doing good; sleeping and waking mean our life in this world, which is earthly, and our life after death, which is spiritual; buying means gaining for ourselves; going to the sellers and buying oil means trying to gain from others after death a love for doing good. Since this could then no longer be done, even though they came to the door of the wedding room with their lamps and the oil they had bought they were told by the bridegroom, "I do not know you." This is because after our life in this world we are still the same kinds of people we were when we were living in this world.

[3] We can see from this that the Lord spoke in pure correspondences; and this is because he was speaking from the divine nature that was within him and that was his own.

That the bridegroom means the Lord; the kingdom of the heavens means the church; the wedding means the marriage of the Lord with the church through good actions that come from love and faith; the young women mean the members of the church; ten means all and five means some; sleeping means an earthly state; buying means gaining for ourselves; the door means admission to heaven; and our not being known by the Lord means our not participating in his love—all this we can conclude on the basis of many passages from the prophetic Word, where these words have similar meanings.

It is because young women mean members of the church that it so often speaks of the virgin and daughter of Zion, of Jerusalem, and of Israel in the prophetic Word. It is because oil means good actions that are done out of love that all the holy utensils of the Israelite church were anointed with oil.

[4] It is much the same in other parables and in all the words that the Lord spoke and that are written in the Gospels. That is why the Lord said that his words were spirit and were life (John 6:63).

It is much the same with all the Lord's miracles, which were divine acts, because they pointed to the various states of people in whom the church was to be established by the Lord. For example, the blind receiving sight meant that people who had been in ignorance of what is true would be given understanding; the deaf being given hearing meant that people who had not listened to the Lord and the Word would hear and obey; the dead being revived meant that people who would otherwise perish spiritually would be brought to life, and so on. This is the meaning of the Lord's answer to the disciples of John when they asked whether he was the one who was to come:

> Tell John the things that you hear and see: the blind are seeing, and the lame are walking; lepers are being cleansed, and the deaf are hearing; the dead are rising again, and the poor are hearing the gospel. (Matthew 11:3, 4, 5)

All the miracles that are recounted in the Word have something in them that involves matters of the Lord, heaven, and the church. That is what makes them divine miracles and distinguishes them from wonders that are not divine.

These few examples are offered by way of illustrating what the spiritual meaning is and showing that it is present throughout the Word and in all its details.

3. *The spiritual meaning is what makes the Word divinely inspired and* **18** *makes every word in it holy.* We hear it said in the church that the Word is holy, but this is because Jehovah God spoke it. However, because people do not see anything holy about it from the letter alone, once they begin to have doubts about its holiness for this reason, then when they read the Word, there is much they can find to justify this attitude. That is,

they think, "Is *this* holy? Is *this* divine?" To prevent this kind of thinking from spreading to more and more people and then gaining strength and so destroying the Lord's union with the church where the Word is, it has now pleased the Lord to unveil the spiritual meaning so that we may know where in the Word that "holy material" lies hidden.

[2] But let me illustrate this too with some examples.

Sometimes the Word talks about Egypt, sometimes about Assyria, sometimes about Edom, Moab, the Ammonites, Tyre and Sidon, and Gog. If we do not know that these names mean matters of heaven and the church, we may be misled and believe that the Word has a lot to say about nations and peoples and only a little about heaven and the church—a lot about earthly matters and not much about heavenly ones. However, if we know what is meant by these nations and peoples or by their names, we can come out of error into truth. [3] By the same token, when we see in the Word the frequent mention of gardens, groves, forests, and their trees, such as olive, grapevine, cedar, poplar, and oak; when we see mention of lambs, sheep, goats, calves, and cattle, as well as mountains, hills, valleys, and their springs, rivers, waters, and so on; if we know nothing about the spiritual meaning of the Word, we can only believe that these and nothing else are the things that they mean. We would not know that garden, grove, and forest mean wisdom, intelligence, and knowledge; that the olive, grapevine, cedar, poplar, and oak mean the heavenly, spiritual, rational, earthly, and sensory types of goodness and truth in the church; that lambs, sheep, goats, calves, and cattle mean innocence, caring, and earthly feelings; that mountains, hills, and valleys mean the higher, lower, and lowest forms of the church; and that Egypt means knowledge, Assyria reasoning, Edom what is earthly, Moab the corruption of what is good, Ammonites the corruption of what is true, Tyre and Sidon the knowledge of what is true and good, and Gog outward worship with no inner content. Once we know this, though, we can think that the Word is about nothing but heavenly matters and that these earthly things are only the vessels that contain them.

[4] But let me illustrate this with another example from the Word. We read in David,

> The voice of Jehovah is upon the waters; the God of glory thunders;
> Jehovah is upon great waters. The voice of Jehovah breaks the cedars.
> Jehovah shatters the cedars of Lebanon. He makes them leap like a calf,
> and Lebanon and Sirion like a young unicorn. The voice of Jehovah

comes down like a flame of fire. The voice of Jehovah makes the wilderness quake; it makes the wilderness of Kadesh quake. The voice of Jehovah makes the deer give birth and strips the woodlands bare, but in his Temple, everyone says, "Glory!" (Psalms 29:3–9)

Anyone who is strictly earthly-minded and does not realize that the details, including every single word here, are holy and divine may say, "What *is* all this—Jehovah sitting on waters, breaking cedars with his voice, making them leap like a calf and Lebanon like a young unicorn, making deer give birth, and so on?" Such people do not realize that spiritually understood, these statements serve as a description of the power of divine truth or the Word. [5] When understood in this way, the "voice of Jehovah" (which here speaks in thunder) means divine truth or the Word in its power. The great waters on which Jehovah sits mean its truths; both the cedars that it breaks and [the cedars of] Lebanon that it shatters mean distortions produced by human reasoning; the calf and the young unicorn mean distortions produced by the earthly and sense-centered self; the flame of fire means the urge to distort; the wilderness and the wilderness of Kadesh mean the church where there is nothing true and nothing good; the deer that the voice of Jehovah causes to give birth mean people who are engaged in doing good on an earthly level; and the woodlands that he strips bare mean the facts and concepts the Word makes accessible to them. That is why it goes on to say that everyone in his Temple says, "Glory!" This means that there are divine truths in the details of the Word, since the temple means the Lord and therefore the Word, as well as heaven and the church, and glory means divine truth.

We can see from all this that there is not a single word in this passage that is not describing the divine power of the Word against all kinds of false beliefs and perceptions in earthly people, and the divine power to reform people.

There is a still deeper level of meaning in the Word, one called *heavenly,* mentioned briefly in §6 above. It is almost impossible to extricate this meaning, though, because it is suited not so much to the thinking of our intellect as to the feelings of our will.

The reason this still deeper meaning (the one called heavenly) is present in the Word is that divine goodness and divine truth emanate from the Lord, divine goodness from his divine love and divine truth from his divine wisdom. Both are present in the Word, since the Word is a divine emanation. And since both are present, the Word brings to life people

19

who read it with reverence. This subject will be discussed, though, under its own heading [§§80–90], where it will be explained that there is a marriage of the Lord and the church in the details of the Word and therefore a marriage of what is good and what is true.

20   4. *The spiritual meaning of the Word has not been recognized before.* It was explained in *Heaven and Hell* 87–105 that absolutely everything in the physical world corresponds to something spiritual, as does absolutely everything in the human body. However, the nature of this correspondence has been unknown until the present time, even though it was common knowledge in ancient times. For the people who lived in those times, the knowledge of how things correspond to each other was the very essence of knowledge. This knowledge was so universal that it governed the writing of all their scrolls and books. [2] The Book of Job, which is an ancient work, is full of correspondences. So were the Egyptian hieroglyphs and the fables of the earliest peoples. All the ancient churches had practices that symbolized heavenly things. Their rituals, as well as the regulations underlying their worship, were made up entirely of correspondences. The same held true for everything about the church among the children of Jacob—their burnt offerings and sacrifices were correspondences even with respect to details. So were the tabernacle and everything in it. So were their feasts—the Feast of Unleavened Bread, the Feast of Tabernacles, the Feast of First Fruits. So too was the priesthood of Aaron and the Levites as well as the sacred garments of Aaron and his sons. So also were all the laws and judgments that had to do with their worship and life. [3] And since divine things become manifest in this world by means of correspondences, the Word was written entirely by means of them. That is why the Lord, speaking as he did from his divine nature, spoke in correspondences, since in the physical world whatever comes from the divine nature clothes itself in things that correspond to divine realities and that therefore conceal in their embrace the divine realities that we call heavenly and spiritual.

21   I have been taught that the people of the earliest church, the one that existed before the Flood, were so heavenly in nature that they talked with angels of heaven, and that they were able to talk with them in correspondences. This meant that their wisdom developed to the point that when they saw anything on earth, they not only thought of it in earthly terms but thought of it in spiritual terms at the same time, and therefore their thoughts joined those of angels.

I have also been taught that Enoch (mentioned in Genesis 5:21–24) and others who joined him collected correspondences from the mouth of these [sages] and passed their knowledge on to their descendants. As a result of this, the knowledge of correspondences was not only familiar but was devotedly practiced in many Middle Eastern countries, especially in the land of Canaan, Egypt, Assyria, Chaldea, Syria, and Arabia; and in Tyre, Sidon, and Nineveh. From coastal locations it was transmitted to Greece. There, however, the knowledge was changed into fables, as we can tell from the writings of the earliest people there.

With the passage of time, though, the symbolic practices of the church, which were correspondences, were turned into idolatrous practices and even into magic. When this happened, the Lord's divine providence saw to it that this knowledge was gradually erased, and among the people of Israel and Judah it became utterly lost and extinct. **22**

The worship of those people, though, was still composed entirely of correspondences, so it represented heavenly realities even though they did not know what they meant. They were in fact completely earthly people and therefore neither wanted to know nor could know anything about spiritual things or, consequently, about correspondences.

The idolatrous practices of the peoples in ancient times arose from their knowledge of correspondences because everything we see on our planet corresponds to something spiritual—not only trees, but also all kinds of animals and birds as well as fish, and so on. The ancients who were devoted to a knowledge of these correspondences made themselves images that corresponded to heavenly realities, and they took pleasure in them because they signified what was happening in heaven and the church. That is why they placed them not only in their temples but in their homes as well—not to be worshiped but to remind them of the heavenly reality signified by these objects. So in Egypt and elsewhere their images looked like calves, oxen, and snakes as well as children, old people, and young women. This is because calves and oxen mean the feelings and drives of the earthly self, snakes the shrewdness of the sensory self, children innocence and caring, old people wisdom, and young women the desire for what is true, and so on. **23**

Because the ancients had placed these images and statues in and around temples, their descendants, after the knowledge of these correspondences had been lost, began to worship the images and statues themselves as sacred, and eventually regarded them as demigods. [2] Much the same happened in other nations—with the Philistines' Dagon in Ashdod, for example (see 1 Samuel 5:1–12). The upper part of Dagon looked human and the lower part looked like a fish, an image devised because a human means intelligence, a fish means knowledge, and intelligence and knowledge become one.

This is also why the ancients' worship was in gardens and groves depending on the species of trees, and on mountains and hills. Gardens and groves meant wisdom and intelligence, and each tree meant some specific aspect of them. Olive trees, for example, meant good actions done out of love; grapevines meant true insights that arise from doing good; cedars meant a rational understanding of what is good and true; mountains meant the highest heaven; and hills meant the heaven below it.

[3] The survival of the knowledge of correspondences until the Coming of the Lord among the greater part of those in the East is demonstrated in the account of the wise men from that region who came to the Lord when he was born—because in that story a star went before them and they bore gifts of gold, frankincense, and myrrh (Matthew 2:1, 2, 9, 10, 11). That is, the star that went before them meant a new insight from heaven; and gold meant what is good on the heavenly level, frankincense what is good on the spiritual level, and myrrh what is good on the earthly level; and these three are the basis of all worship.

[4] There was no knowledge at all of correspondences among the people of Israel and Judah, however, even though correspondence was the sole basis of all their worship, all the judgments and statutes given them through Moses, and all the contents of the Word. This was because they were idolatrous at heart, so much so that they did not even want to know that any element of their worship had a heavenly or spiritual meaning. That is, they wanted all these things to be holy in and of themselves and just for them, so if they had noticed anything heavenly and spiritual, they not only would have rejected it but would have profaned it as well. For this reason heaven was closed to them, so closed that they were scarcely aware that there was such a thing as eternal life. The truth of this is obvious from the fact that they did not recognize the Lord even though the whole Sacred Scripture prophesied about him and predicted him. The sole reason they rejected him was that he taught people about a heavenly kingdom and not an earthly one. That is, they wanted a Messiah who would raise them to supremacy over all the nations in the whole world and not some Messiah who would be concerned with their eternal salvation.

Further, they assert that the Word contains in itself many secrets that they call mystical, but they do not want those secrets to be about the Lord. They do want to know them, though, when they are told that they are about gold.

The reason the knowledge of correspondences that gives access to the **24** spiritual meaning of the Word was not discerned in later times was that the people of the early Christian church were quite uneducated, so this knowledge could not be revealed to them. That is, if it had been revealed it would have been of no use to them and they would not have understood it.

After those times, darkness spread over the whole Christian world as a consequence of papal rule; and the people who relied on papal authority and convinced themselves of its falsities neither could nor wanted to accept anything spiritual, including the correspondence of earthly things with spiritual things in the Word. If they had, they would have realized that Peter does not mean Peter but the Lord as the Rock. They would also have realized that the Word is divine all the way to its very heart and that a papal decree is of no importance by comparison.

After the Reformation heavenly truths were hidden away, because people began to differentiate between faith and caring and to worship God in three persons and therefore to worship three gods whom they thought were one; and if heavenly truths had been discovered, people would have distorted them and brought them down to the level of faith alone. They would not have associated any of those truths with caring and love, so they would have shut themselves out of heaven.

The reason the spiritual meaning of the Word has now been unveiled **25** by the Lord is that a body of teaching based on genuine truth has now been revealed, and this teaching and no other is in harmony with the spiritual meaning of the Word.

That spiritual meaning is indicated by the appearing of the Lord in the clouds of heaven with glory and power in Matthew 24:30, the chapter dealing with the close of the age, which is to be understood as the last time of the church.

Then too, the opening of the Word with respect to its spiritual meaning was promised in the Book of Revelation. That is what is meant there by the white horse and the great supper to which all were invited (Revelation 19:11–18). Chapter 19 also tells us that the spiritual meaning would not be recognized for a long time, at least by people mired in false teachings (especially about the Lord) and therefore closed to truth. That is the meaning of the beast and the monarchs of the earth in Revelation who were going to make war with the one who sat on the white horse (Revelation 19:19). The beast means Roman Catholics (see Revelation 17:3), and the monarchs of the earth mean Protestants who are mired in false theological principles.

26

5. *From now on the spiritual meaning of the Word can be given only to people who are focused on genuine truths that come from the Lord.* This is because we cannot see the spiritual meaning unless we are given it by the Lord alone and unless we focus on genuine truths from him. The spiritual meaning of the Word is all about the Lord and his kingdom, and is the meaning that engages his angels in heaven. It is actually his divine truth there. We can do violence to it if we have some knowledge of correspondences and try to use that knowledge to explore the spiritual meaning of the Word with our own brain power. This is because we can distort that meaning with the few correspondences familiar to us and twist them to support what is actually false. This would be doing violence to both divine truth and heaven. So if our efforts to open that meaning come from ourselves and not from the Lord, heaven is closed to us; and once it is closed, we either see nothing or lose our spiritual sanity.

[2] Another reason is that the Lord teaches everyone by means of the Word; and he teaches using the truths that we have and does not pour new truths directly in. This means that if we are not focused on divine truths or if the few we have are tangled in distortions, we can use these few to distort truths. This, as is commonly known, is what happens with heretics in their use of the literal sense of the Word. So to keep anyone from gaining access to the spiritual meaning of the Word or from distorting the genuine truth of that meaning, the Lord has stationed the guards meant in the Word by the angel guardians.

[3] This is how the stationing of those guardians was represented to me:

> I was shown some big purses that looked like bags, in which an ample supply of silver was stored; and since they were open, it seemed as though anyone could take out the silver stored in them—could in fact steal it. However, there were two angels sitting near the purses, serving as guards. The place where the purses were stored looked like a manger in a stable. In a nearby room I could see some modest young women together with a chaste wife. There were two little children standing near the room. I was told that I was to play with them, but wisely, not childishly. After that a prostitute appeared, and then a horse lying dead.

[4] After I had seen all this, I was told that this scene represented the literal meaning of the Word in which spiritual meaning was contained. The big purses full of silver meant an abundant supply of knowledge about what is true. Their being open but guarded by angels meant that anyone could draw knowledge of truth from them but care had to be taken to prevent anyone from distorting the spiritual meaning, in which there was nothing but truths. The manger in the stable where the purses were meant spiritual teaching for the sake of our understanding. That is what a manger means because horses, which eat from mangers, mean an understanding. [5] The modest young women whom I saw in the nearby room meant desire for what is true, and the chaste wife meant the union of good actions and truth. The little children meant an innocence of wisdom within. They were angels from the third heaven, all of whom look like little children. The prostitute with the dead horse meant the distortion of the Word by so many people nowadays, a distortion that leads to the death of all understanding of truth—the prostitute meaning the distortion and the dead horse the total absence of any understanding of truth.

The Literal Meaning of the Word
Is the Foundation, the Container, and the Support
of Its Spiritual and Heavenly Meanings

IN every work of God there is something first, something intermediate, and something last; and what is first works through what is intermediate to what is last and in this way becomes manifest and persists, so what is last is a *foundation*. The first is also in the intermediate, and through the intermediate is in what is last, so what is last is a *container;* and since what is last is a container and a foundation, it is also a *support.*

    The learned world understands that this *series of three* can be called a goal, the means to it, and its result, as well as being, becoming, and

27

28

achieving full manifestation. Being is the goal, becoming is the means, and achieving full manifestation is the result. This means that there is a series of three in everything that is complete—a series called first, intermediate, and last; or goal, means, and result; or being, becoming, and achieving full manifestation.

Once this is understood we can also understand that every work of God is complete and perfect in its final stage and also that the whole, which is a series of three, is in the final stage, because the prior stages are together in it.

29 This is why *three* in the Word spiritually understood means complete, perfect, and all together; and since this is its meaning it is used in the Word whenever anything is so described, as in the following instances:

Isaiah went naked and barefoot *for three years* (Isaiah 20:3). Jehovah called Samuel *three times,* Samuel ran to Eli *three times,* and *the third time* Eli understood what was happening (1 Samuel 3:1–8). David told Jonathan that he would hide in the field *for three days;* later Jonathan shot *three arrows* beside the rock; and after that David bowed down to Jonathan *three times* (1 Samuel 20:5, 12–41). Elijah stretched himself out on the widow's son *three times* (1 Kings 17:21). Elijah ordered people to pour water over a burnt offering *three times* (1 Kings 18:34). Jesus said that the kingdom of the heavens was like yeast, which a woman took and hid in *three measures* [of flour] until it was all leavened (Matthew 13:33). Jesus said to Peter that Peter would deny him *three times* (Matthew 26:34). The Lord said to Peter *three times,* "Do you love me?" (John 21:15, 16, 17). Jonah was in the belly of the whale *three days and three nights* (Jonah 1:17). Jesus said that they would destroy the Temple, and he would build it in *three days* (Matthew 26:61). Jesus prayed *three times* in Gethsemane (Matthew 26:39–44). Jesus rose *on the third day* (Matthew 28:1).

There are many other passages where threes are mentioned, and they are mentioned when it is a matter of something finished and completed, because that is what this number means.

30 This is by way of preface to what follows, so that the discussion there can readily be understood; the point being to demonstrate that the earthly meaning of the Word, which is its literal meaning, is the foundation, container, and support of its spiritual and heavenly meanings.

31 It was noted in §§6 and 19 above that there are three levels of meaning in the Word and that the heavenly meaning is its first level, the spiritual meaning its intermediate level, and the earthly meaning its last level. This enables anyone who thinks rationally to conclude that the first level of the Word, the heavenly, works through its intermediate, which is the spiritual, to the last level, which is the earthly. We can also conclude that the last level is therefore a *foundation.* We can conclude further that the first level (the heavenly) is within the intermediate level (the spiritual), and through this in the last level (the earthly), which means that the last level (the earthly), which is the literal meaning of the Word, is a *container;* and since it is a container and a foundation, it is also a *support.*

However, there is no way to explain briefly how this happens. These are mysteries familiar to heaven's angels that will be unfolded—as far as possible—in the treatises listed in the preface to *Teachings on the Lord: Angelic Wisdom about Divine Providence; Angelic Wisdom about Omnipotence, Omnipresence, and Omniscience; Angelic Wisdom about Divine Love and Wisdom;* and *Angelic Wisdom about Life.* **32**

The Word is essentially a divine work for the salvation of the human race. For present purposes, it will suffice to conclude from what has been said above that the Word's last level of meaning (which is earthly and is called "the literal meaning") is a foundation, container, and support for its two deeper levels of meaning.

It follows from all this that without its literal meaning the Word would be like a palace without a foundation, like a castle in the air. The only thing on the ground would be its shadow, and shadows disappear. The Word without its literal meaning would be like a temple containing an abundance of holy objects, with a central inner sanctum, but without a roof or walls to contain them. If these were lacking or were taken away, its holy contents would be plundered by thieves or torn apart by the beasts of the earth and the birds of heaven, and would therefore be scattered far and wide. **33**

By the same token, it would be like the tabernacle's inmost area, which housed the ark of the covenant, and its middle area, which housed the golden lampstand, the golden altar of incense, and the table with the showbread on it—all its holy contents—without the curtains and veils that surrounded them.

The Word without its literal meaning would be like a human body without the coverings called layers of skin and without the structural supports called bones. Lacking both of these, all the internal organs would spill out.

Then too, it would be like the heart and lungs in the chest without the covering called the pleura and the framework called the rib cage, or like the brain without its specific covering called the dura mater or its general covering, container, and support called the skull.

That is what the Word would be like without its literal meaning, which is why it says in Isaiah that Jehovah creates a covering over all glory (Isaiah 4:5).

34 It would be the same for the heavens where angels live if it were not for the world where we live. We, as human beings, are their foundation, container, and support, and we have the Word with us and in us.

Overall, the heavens are divided into two kingdoms, which are called the heavenly kingdom and the spiritual kingdom. These two kingdoms are founded upon the earthly kingdom where we live. A similar structure exists in the Word, which we have with us and in us.

See *Heaven and Hell* 20–28 on the division of the angelic heavens into two kingdoms, a heavenly one and a spiritual one.

35 *Teachings on the Lord* 28 shows that the Old Testament prophets represented the Lord in respect to the Word and therefore meant the teaching of the church drawn from the Word, and that because of this they were addressed as "children of humanity." It follows from this that by the various things they suffered and endured they represented the violence done to the literal meaning of the Word by Jews. Isaiah, for example, took the sackcloth off his waist and the sandals off his feet and went naked and barefoot for three years (Isaiah 20:2, 3). Similarly, Ezekiel the prophet took a barber's razor to his head and his beard, burned a third of the hair in the middle of the city, struck a third with a sword, and scattered a third to the wind; also, he bound a few hairs in his hems and eventually threw a few into the midst of a fire and burned them (Ezekiel 5:1–4).

Since the prophets represented the Word and therefore meant the teaching of the church drawn from the Word (as just noted), and since the head means wisdom from the Word, the hair and the beard mean the outermost form of truth. It is because of this meaning that inflicting *baldness* on yourself was a sign of immense grief and being discovered to be *bald* was an immense disgrace. This and this alone is why the prophet shaved off his hair and his beard—to represent the state of the Jewish church in regard to the Word. This and this alone is why two she-bears tore apart forty-two boys *who called Elisha bald* (2 Kings 2:23, 24, 25)— because as just noted the prophet represented the Word, and his baldness signified the Word without an outermost meaning.

We shall see in §49 below that the Nazirites represented the Lord's Word in its outermost forms, which is why they were commanded to let their hair grow and not to shave any of it. In Hebrew, "Nazirite" actually means "hair." It was commanded also that the high priest was not to shave his head (Leviticus 21:10) and that the fathers of their families as well were not to do so (Leviticus 21:5).

That is why they regarded baldness as such an immense disgrace, as we can tell from the following passages:

There will be baldness upon all heads, and every beard will be cut off. (Isaiah 15:2; Jeremiah 48:37)

There will be shame upon all faces and baldness on all heads. (Ezekiel 7:18)

Every head was made bald and every shoulder hairless. (Ezekiel 29:18)

I will put sackcloth around all waists and baldness upon every head. (Amos 8:10)

Make yourself bald and cut off your hair because of your precious children; make yourself still more bald, because they have left you and gone into exile. (Micah 1:16)

Here making yourself bald and making yourself still more bald means distorting truths of the Word in its outermost forms. Once they have been distorted, as was done by Jews, the whole Word is ruined, because the outermost forms of the Word are what it rests on and what holds it up. In fact, every word in it is a base and support for the Word's heavenly and spiritual truths.

Since a head of hair means truth in its outermost forms, in the spiritual world everyone who trivializes the Word and distorts its literal meaning looks bald; but those who respect and love it have good-looking hair. On this, see §49 below.

The Word in its outermost or earthly meaning, which is its literal meaning, is also meant by the wall of the holy Jerusalem, which was made of jasper, by the foundations of the wall, which were precious stones, as well as by the gates, which were pearls (Revelation 21:18–21). This is because Jerusalem means the church in regard to its teachings. There will be more on this, though, under the next heading [§43]. We may now conclude from what has been presented that the literal meaning of the

36

Word, which is earthly, is the foundation, container, and support of its inner meanings, which are a spiritual meaning and a heavenly meaning.

Divine Truth,
in All Its Fullness, Holiness, and Power,
Is Present in the Literal Meaning of the Word

37 THE reason the Word is in its fullness, holiness, and power in the literal meaning is that the two prior or deeper meanings that are called spiritual and heavenly are together in the earthly meaning, which is the literal meaning, as explained in §31 above. Now I need to state briefly how they are together.

38 In heaven and in the world we find sequential arrangement and simultaneous arrangement. In sequential arrangement, one thing replaces and follows another, from the highest to the lowest. In simultaneous arrangement, though, one thing adjoins another, from the innermost to the outermost. The sequential arrangement is like a column with steps from top to bottom, while the simultaneous arrangement is like a composite object that forms a series of concentric circles [that radiate] from its center to its outer surfaces.

Next I need to explain how the sequential arrangement comes to be a simultaneous arrangement on the outermost level. It comes about like this. The highest elements of the sequential arrangement become the innermost elements of the simultaneous arrangement, and the lowest elements of the sequential arrangement become the outermost elements of the simultaneous arrangement. It is as though the column of steps collapsed and became a tightly fitted body on one level.

[2] That is how the sequential becomes the simultaneous; and this holds for absolutely everything in the earthly world and absolutely everything in the spiritual world, since there is something first, something

intermediate, and something last everywhere, and what is first stretches toward its final form, passing through what is intermediate to reach it. Now for the Word. What is heavenly, what is spiritual, and what is earthly emanate from the Lord sequentially, and they exist on the last level in a simultaneous arrangement. This means that now the heavenly and spiritual meanings of the Word are together within its earthly meaning.

Once this is grasped, we can see how the earthly meaning of the Word, which is its literal meaning, is the foundation, container, and support of its spiritual and heavenly meanings, and how divine goodness and divine truth are present in their fullness, holiness, and power in the literal meaning of the Word.

We can tell from this that in its literal meaning the Word is really the Word. There is spirit and life within; the spiritual meaning is its spirit and the heavenly meaning is its life. This is what the Lord said: "The words that I speak to you are spirit and are life" (John 6:63). The Lord said his words to the world and said them in their earthly meaning. **39**

Apart from the earthly meaning, which is the literal meaning, the spiritual and heavenly meanings are not the Word; [without it] they are like a spirit and life without a body—and as just noted in §33, like a palace that has no foundation to rest on.

To a considerable extent, the truths of the literal meaning of the Word are not bare truths but are semblances of truth; like similes and comparisons, they are drawn from the kinds of things that are in the physical world and are therefore adapted and fitted to the comprehension of uneducated people and children. Since they are correspondences, though, they are receptacles and dwelling places for genuine truth, like containers that gather in and hold something the way a crystal goblet holds a fine wine, or a silver plate holds gourmet food. They are like garments that serve as clothing, whether swaddling clothes for babies or attractive dresses for young women. They are also like the information in the earthly mind that comprehends within itself the perceptions of the spiritual self and its affection for truth. **40**

The actual bare truths that are gathered in, contained, clothed, and comprehended are in the Word's spiritual meaning; and the bare goodness is in its heavenly meaning.

[2] However, this needs illustrations from the Word. Jesus said,

Woe to you, scribes and Pharisees, because you cleanse the outside of the cup and the plate, but inside they are full of extortion and excess.

Blind Pharisee, cleanse the inside of the cup and the plate first, so that
the outside of them may be clean as well. (Matthew 23:25, 26)

The Lord said this using terms from the outermost level, which serve as
containers. He said "the cup and the plate"—the cup meaning wine and
the wine meaning the truth contained in the Word, the plate meaning
food and the food meaning the goodness contained in the Word. Cleansing the inside of the cup and the plate means purifying what lies within
us, matters of our will and thought and therefore of our love and faith,
by means of the Word. The outside becoming clean by cleansing the
inside means the consequent purification of our outer selves—our actions
and speech, that is, since these have their essence from what lies within.

[3] Again, Jesus said,

There was a certain rich man who was clothed in purple and fine linen
and indulged himself in glorious feasting every day; and there was a
poor man named Lazarus, full of sores, who was laid on his doorstep.
(Luke 16:19, 20)

Here too the Lord was speaking in earthly terms that were correspondences and that contained spiritual realities. The rich man means the Jewish people, who are called "rich" because they have the Word, in which
there is spiritual wealth. The purple and fine linen of his clothing means
what is good and true in the Word, the purple meaning what is good in
it, and the fine linen what is true. Indulging in glorious feasting every day
means a delight in owning and reading it. The poor man Lazarus means
the Gentiles who did not have the Word. Their being scorned and rejected
by the Jews is meant by Lazarus being full of sores and laid on the rich
man's doorstep.

[4] The reason Lazarus means Gentiles is that the Lord loved Gentiles the way the Lord loved the Lazarus whom he raised from the dead
(John 11:3, 5, 36), who was called his friend (John 11:11), and who reclined
with him at meals (John 12:2).

We can see from these two passages that the true and good statements of the literal meaning of the Word are like containers and clothing
for the bare truths and goodness that lie hidden in the spiritual and heavenly meaning of the Word.

41 Since that is what the Word is like in its literal meaning, it follows that
readers who are seeking divine truths see divine truths in an earthly light
when they are reading the Word in enlightenment from the Lord, provided their faith is that at heart the Word is divinely holy; and especially if

they have a basic trust that this quality of the Word is the result of its spiritual and heavenly meaning. This is because heaven's light, the light that shows us the spiritual meaning of the Word, flows into the earthly light that shows us the literal meaning of the Word and enlightens that mental function that we call our reasoning powers, causing them to see and recognize where divine truths stand out and where they lie hidden. These insights flow in with heaven's light for some people, sometimes even when they are not aware of it.

Since at the heart of its inmost level our Word is like a flame that ignites us because of its heavenly meaning, and since at the heart of its intermediate level it is like a light that enlightens us because of its spiritual meaning, at the heart of its outermost level it is like a ruby and a diamond because of its earthly meaning, which contains both of the deeper ones. It is like a ruby because of its heavenly flame and like a diamond because of its spiritual light.

42

Since that is the nature of the Word in its literal meaning because of the way light shines through it, the Word's literal meaning is meant by *the foundations of the wall of Jerusalem* [Revelation 21:14, 19], by *the Urim and Thummim* of Aaron's breastplate [Exodus 28:30; Leviticus 8:8], by the *Garden of Eden* where the king of Tyre lived [Ezekiel 28:12–13], as well as by *the curtains and veils of the tabernacle* [Exodus 26:1–13; 36:8–17] and the *decorated surfaces inside the Jerusalem temple* [1 Kings 6–7]; while the Word in its essential glory is meant by *the Lord when he was transfigured* [Matthew 17:2; Mark 9:2].

As for *the truths of the literal meaning of the Word being meant by the foundations of the wall of the New Jerusalem in Revelation 21,* this follows from the fact that the New Jerusalem means a new church in regard to its teachings, as demonstrated in *Teachings on the Lord* 63 and 64. So the wall and its foundations must mean the outer level of the Word, which is its literal meaning. This, in fact, is the source of each body of teaching, and through that body of teaching, the source of the church; and it is like a wall with its foundations, which encloses and protects the city.

43

This is what we read in Revelation about the wall of the New Jerusalem and its foundations:

> The angel measured the wall of the city Jerusalem: one hundred and forty-four cubits, which is the measure of a human being, that is, of an angel. And the wall had twelve foundations, adorned with precious stones of every kind. The first foundation was jasper, the second sapphire,

the third chalcedony, the fourth emerald, the fifth onyx, the sixth sardius, the seventh chrysolite, the eighth beryl, the ninth topaz, the tenth chrysoprase, the eleventh jacinth, and the twelfth amethyst. (Revelation 21:17, 18, 19, 20)

The number one hundred and forty-four means all the true and good elements of the church that arise from its teachings, which are drawn from the literal meaning of the Word. Twelve means much the same. A human being means understanding; an angel means divine truth as the source of understanding; the measure means the quality of that [understanding and truth]; the wall and its foundations mean the literal meaning of the Word; precious stones mean the elements of truth and goodness contained and carefully arranged in the Word, which are the source of a body of teaching and through that teaching, the source of the church.

44 *The good and true elements of the literal meaning of the Word are meant by the Urim and Thummim.*

The Urim and Thummim were on the ephod of Aaron, whose priesthood represented the Lord's divine goodness and his work of salvation. The sacred garments of priesthood represented the divine truth that arises from divine goodness. The ephod represented divine truth in its outermost form and therefore the Word in its literal meaning because this, as noted above [§§1–4, 6, 27–36, 38], is divine truth in its outermost form. So the twelve precious stones with the names of the twelve tribes of Israel, which were the Urim and Thummim, mean the complete assemblage of divine truths arising from divine goodness. [2] This is what we read in Moses:

They shall make an ephod of blue, purple, and double-dyed scarlet [thread], and fine woven linen. Then they shall make a breastplate of judgment matching the work of the ephod. And you shall put settings of stones in it, four rows of stones: carnelian, topaz, and emerald, the first row; chrysoprase, sapphire, and diamond, the second row; jacinth, agate, and amethyst, the third row; and beryl, sardius, and jasper, the fourth row. The stones shall have the names of the sons of Israel, [like] the engravings of a signet, each one with its own name; they shall be according to the twelve tribes. Aaron shall wear the Urim and Thummim on the breastplate of judgment, and they shall be over Aaron's heart when he goes in before Jehovah. (Exodus 28:6, 15–21, 30)

[3] I have explained in the appropriate chapter of *Secrets of Heaven* [§§9819–9966] the meaning of Aaron's garments—the ephod, the robe, the tunic, the turban, and the belt. There it is shown that the ephod represented

divine truth in its outermost form; the precious stones represented truths from which light shines because they teach what is good; the twelve precious stones represented all the truths, in the right arrangement, that shine in their outermost form because good actions from love are what they teach; the twelve tribes of Israel represented all aspects of the church; the breastplate represented divine truth that comes from divine goodness; and the Urim and Thummim represented the radiance of divine truth that comes from divine goodness, in its outermost forms. In fact, in the language of angels, "Urim" means shining fire and "Thummim" means radiance. (In Hebrew the latter means "wholeness".) It is also shown there that oracular answers were given by variations in the light accompanied by silently projected ideas or even by words that resounded aloud, and other methods.

[4] We can conclude from this that the precious stones also meant truths in the outermost meaning of the Word that come from goodness; and this is the only way oracular answers are given from heaven, because that is the meaning in which the emanating divine is fully present. By seeing precious stones and diamonds among angels and spirits in the spiritual world, I have been able to see very clearly that precious stones and diamonds mean divine truths in their outermost forms, like the truths in the literal meaning of the Word. I have seen angels wearing them and have seen gems in their jewel boxes. I have also been granted to know that they correspond to truths in outermost form—in fact, this correspondence is what causes these precious stones and diamonds to exist and to look the way they do.

Since this is what diamonds and precious stones mean, John also saw them on the head of the dragon (Revelation 12:3), on the horns of the beast (Revelation 13:1), and on the whore who was sitting on the scarlet beast (Revelation 17:4). He saw them on these creatures because they meant the people of the Christian church, who have the Word.

Truths of the literal meaning of the Word are meant by the precious **45** *stones in the Garden of Eden where the king of Tyre was said to live, according to Ezekiel.*

We read in Ezekiel,

> O king of Tyre, you had sealed your full measure and were full of wisdom and perfect in beauty. You were in Eden, the garden of God. Every precious stone was your covering—ruby, topaz, and diamond; beryl, sardonyx, and jasper; sapphire, chrysoprase, and emerald; and gold. (Ezekiel 28:12, 13)

Tyre in the Word means knowledge of what is true and what is good; a king means what is true in the church; the Garden of Eden means wisdom and understanding from the Word; precious stones mean truths from which light shines because they teach what is good—the kind we have in the literal meaning of the Word—and since this is what these stones mean, they are called its covering. On the literal meaning as the covering of the deeper levels of the Word, see under the preceding heading [§33; see also §40].

46 *The literal meaning of the Word is symbolized by the veils and curtains of the tabernacle.*

The tabernacle represented heaven and the church, which is why its form was outlined by Jehovah on Mount Sinai. Because of this, everything in the tabernacle—the lampstands, the golden altar of incense, the table for the showbread—represented and therefore referred to holy matters of heaven and the church; and the most holy place, where the ark of the covenant was, represented and therefore referred to the very heart of heaven and the church. Further, the actual law written on the two stone tablets and kept in the ark meant the Lord as the Word. Now, since outer things get their essence from inner things, and both outer and inner things get their essence from the very center, which in this instance was the law, everything in the tabernacle also represented and referred to the holy contents of the Word. It then follows that the outermost features of the tabernacle, the veils and curtains that were coverings and enclosures, meant the outermost features of the Word, which are the true and good elements of its literal meaning. Because this is what they meant, *all the curtains and veils were made of fine linen tightly woven, and of blue, purple, and double-dyed scarlet [thread], [and were embroidered] with angel guardians* (Exodus 26:1, 31, 36).

The general and specific symbolism and meaning of the tabernacle and everything in it has been explained in the treatment of this chapter in *Secrets of Heaven* [9593–9692]. It is explained there that the curtains and veils represented outward features of the church and therefore also outward features of the Word. The linen or fine linen meant truth of a spiritual origin, blue meant truth of a heavenly origin, purple meant heavenly goodness, double-dyed scarlet meant spiritual goodness, and angel guardians meant protection for the inner contents of the Word.

47 *The outer attributes of the Word, which are its literal meaning, are represented by the decorated surfaces inside the Jerusalem temple.*

This is because the Temple in Jerusalem represented the same things as the tabernacle did—heaven and the church, that is, and therefore also the Word.

The Lord himself tells us in John that the Temple in Jerusalem meant his divine-human nature:

> "Destroy this temple, and in three days I will raise it up." He was speaking of the temple of his body. (John 2:19, 21)

And when something means the Lord it also means the Word, because the Lord is the Word. Now, since the inner contents of the Temple represented the inner attributes of heaven and of the church and therefore of the Word as well, so too the decorated surfaces inside the Temple represented and referred to the outer attributes of heaven and of the church and therefore of the Word as well, which are the elements of its literal meaning.

We read of the Temple and its decorated surfaces inside that it was built of whole uncut stones and was paneled on the inside with cedar, and that all its interior walls were carved with angel guardians, palm trees, and open flowers, and its floor was overlaid with gold (1 Kings 6:7, 9, 29, 30), all referring to the outer attributes of the Word, which are the holy features of its literal meaning.

The Word in its glory was represented by the Lord when he was transfigured. **48**
We read of the Lord, when he was transfigured in the presence of Peter, James, and John, that his face shone like the sun and his clothing became like light; that Moses and Elijah appeared, talking with him; that a bright cloud overshadowed the disciples; and that a voice was heard coming from the cloud, saying, "This is my beloved Son. Hear him" (Matthew 17:1–5).

I have been taught that at this time the Lord represented the Word. His face, which shone like the sun, represented his divine goodness; his clothing, which became like light, represented his divine truth; Moses and Elijah represented the historical and prophetic books of the Word—Moses, broadly, the books written by him and by extension the historical books, and Elijah the books of the prophets; the bright cloud that overshadowed the disciples meant the Word in its literal meaning. So it was from this that they heard the voice say, "This is my beloved Son. Hear him." This is because all proclamations and answers from heaven, without exception, come about by means of outermost forms, the kind we find in the literal meaning of the Word; they come about in fullness by means of the Lord.

49 Up to this point I have shown that in its earthly or literal meaning the Word is in its holiness and fullness. I now need to explain that in its literal meaning the Word is also in its *power.*

You can tell the amount and the nature of the power of divine truth both in the heavens and on earth from what has been said about the power of heaven's angels in *Heaven and Hell* 228–233. The power of divine truth is exercised primarily against whatever is false and evil and therefore against the hells. These need to be resisted by the use of truths from the literal meaning of the Word. The Lord also has power to save us by means of whatever truth we have, because we are reformed and reborn by means of truths from the literal meaning of the Word; and we are then rescued from hell and brought into heaven. The Lord assumed this power in his divine-human nature as well after he fulfilled all things of the Word even to the last. [2] That is why the Lord said to the chief priest, when he was about to fulfill what remained by suffering on the cross, "Hereafter you will see the Son of Humanity sitting at the right hand of power and coming in the clouds of heaven" (Matthew 26:64; Mark 14:62). The Son of Humanity is the Lord as the Word; the clouds of heaven are the Word in its literal meaning; sitting at the right hand of God is omnipotence by means of the Word (see also Mark 16:19).

In the Jewish church, the Lord's power through the outermost forms of truth was represented by the Nazirites and by Samson, who is described as a Nazirite from his mother's womb and whose power was associated with his hair, "Nazirite" and "Naziriteship" also mean hair. [3] Samson made this clear when he said, "No razor has come upon my head, because I [have been] a Nazirite from my mother's womb. If I am shorn, then my strength will leave me and I will become weak, and will be like anyone else" (Judges 16:17). No one could know why Naziriteship with its reference to hair was instituted, and therefore why Samson got his strength from his hair, except by knowing the meaning a head has in the Word. Heads mean the heavenly wisdom angels and people receive from the Lord by means of divine truth. So the hair of the head means heavenly wisdom in its outermost forms and also divine truth in its outermost forms.

[4] Since this is the meaning of hair because of its correspondence with heavenly realities, the command to the Nazirites was that they should not shave the hair of their heads, because this was the Naziriteship of God upon their heads (Numbers 6:1–21); so there was also the command that the high

priest and his sons were not to shave their heads or they would die and wrath would fall upon the whole house of Israel (Leviticus 10:6).

[5] Since hair was holy because of this meaning (which comes from its correspondence), the Son of Humanity, the Lord as the Word, was described as having hair that "was white like wool, as white as snow" (Revelation 1:14), and something similar is said of the Ancient of Days (Daniel 7:9). See also what is said on this subject in §35 above.

In short, divine truth or the Word has power in the literal meaning because that is where the Word is in its fullness and because that is where angels from both of the Lord's kingdoms come together with people in this world.

The Church's Body of Teaching
Is to Be Drawn from the Literal Meaning of the Word
and Is to Be Supported by It

THE preceding chapter [§§37–49] was devoted to showing that in its literal meaning the Word is in its fullness, holiness, and power; and since the Lord is the Word (because he is everything in the Word), it follows that the Lord is most present in that meaning and that he teaches and enlightens us through it. **50**

I need to present this, though, in the following sequence.

1. The Word is not understandable without a body of teaching.
2. A body of teaching must be drawn from the literal meaning of the Word.
3. However, the divine truth that a body of teaching should have can be seen only when we are being enlightened by the Lord.

1. *The Word is not understandable without a body of teaching.* This is because in its literal meaning the Word is entirely made up of correspondences, to allow spiritual and heavenly matters to be gathered within it in such a way that each word can be their container and support. That is **51**

why in many passages the literal meaning is not made up of bare truths but of clothed truths, which we may call semblances of truth. Many of them are adapted to the comprehension of ordinary people who do not raise their thoughts above what they can see with their eyes. There are other passages where there seem to be contradictions, though there are no contradictions in the Word when it is seen in its own light. Then too, there are places in the prophets where we find collections of personal names and place-names that make no sense to us—see the examples in §15 above.

Since that is what the literal meaning of the Word is like, it stands to reason that it cannot be understood without a body of teaching.

[2] Some examples may serve to illustrate this. It says that Jehovah repents (Exodus 32:12, 14; Jonah 3:9; 4:2). It also says that Jehovah does not repent (Numbers 23:19; 1 Samuel 15:29). Without a body of teaching, these statements do not agree.

It says that Jehovah visits the iniquities of the parents on the children to the third and fourth generation (Numbers 14:18), and it says that parents will not be put to death for their children and children will not be put to death for their parents, but each will die in his or her own sin (Deuteronomy 24:16). Seen in the light of a body of teaching, these statements do not disagree but agree.

[3] Jesus said,

> Ask, and it will be given to you; seek, and you will find; knock, and it will be opened to you. Everyone who asks receives, those who seek find, and to those who knock it will be opened. (Matthew 7:7, 8; 21:21, 22)

In the absence of a body of teaching, people would believe that everyone's request is granted, but a body of teaching yields the belief that we are given whatever we ask if we ask it not on our own behalf but on the Lord's. That is in fact what the Lord tells us:

> If you abide in me and my words abide in you, you will ask for whatever you want and it will be done for you. (John 15:7)

[4] The Lord says "Blessed are the poor, because theirs is the kingdom of God" (Luke 6:20). Without a body of teaching, we might think that heaven belongs to the poor and not to the rich. A body of teaching instructs us, though, that this means those who are poor *in spirit,* for the Lord said,

> Blessed are the poor in spirit, because theirs is the kingdom of the heavens. (Matthew 5:3)

[5] The Lord says,

Do not judge, or you will be judged; with the same judgment you pass [on others] you yourself will be judged. (Matthew 7:1, 2; Luke 6:37)

In the absence of a body of teaching, this could be used to support the assertion that we should not say that an evil act is evil or judge that an evil person is evil. A body of teaching, though, tells us that it is permissible to pass judgment if we do so in an upright, righteous way. In fact, the Lord says,

Judge with righteous judgment. (John 7:24)

[6] Jesus says,

Do not be called teacher, because one is your Teacher: Christ. You should not call anyone on earth your father, because you have one Father, and he is in the heavens. You should not be called masters, because one is your Master: Christ. (Matthew 23:8, 9, 10)

In the absence of a body of teaching, it would turn out that it was wrong to call anyone a teacher or a father or a master; but from a body of teaching we come to know that this is permissible in an earthly sense but not in a spiritual sense.

[7] Jesus said to the disciples,

When the Son of Humanity sits on the throne of his glory, you will also sit on twelve thrones, judging the twelve tribes of Israel. (Matthew 19:28)

These words could lead us to believe that the Lord's disciples will be passing judgment, when quite the contrary, they cannot judge anyone. So a body of teaching unveils this mystery by explaining that only the Lord, who is omniscient and knows the hearts of all, will judge and can judge, and that his twelve disciples mean the church in the sense of all the true and good principles that it has received from the Lord through the Word. A body of teaching leads us to the conclusion that these principles will judge everyone, which follows from what the Lord says in John 3:17, 18 and 12:47, 48.

[8] People who read the Word without the aid of a body of teaching do not know how to make sense out of what it says in the prophets about the Jewish nation and Jerusalem, namely, that the church will abide in

that nation and that its seat will be in that city forever. Take the following statements, for example.

> Jehovah will visit his flock, the house of Judah, and transform them into a glorious war horse; from Judah will come the cornerstone, from Judah the tent peg, from Judah the battle bow. (Zechariah 10:3, 4)

> Behold, I am coming to dwell in your midst. Jehovah will make Judah his inheritance and will again choose Jerusalem. (Zechariah 2:10, 11, 12)

> On that day it will happen that the mountains will drip with new wine and the hills will flow with milk; and Judah will abide forever, and Jerusalem from generation to generation. (Joel 3:18, 20)

> Behold, the days are coming in which I will sow the house of Israel and the house of Judah with the seed of humankind, and in which I will make a new covenant with the house of Israel and with the house of Judah. This will be the covenant: I will put my law in their midst and I will write it on their heart, and I will become their God and they will become my people. (Jeremiah 31:27, 31, 33)

> On that day ten men from every language of the nations will take hold of the hem of a man of Judah and say, "We will go with you, because we have heard that God is with you." (Zechariah 8:23)

There are other passages of the same nature, such as Isaiah 44:24, 26; 49:22, 23; 65:18; 66:20, 22; Jeremiah 3:18; 23:5; 50:19, 20; Nahum 1:15; Malachi 3:4. In these passages the subject is the Lord's Coming and what will happen at that time.

[9] However, it says something very different in any number of other passages, of which I will cite only the following:

> I will hide my face from them. I will see what their posterity is, for they are a perverse generation, children in whom there is no faithfulness. I have said, "I will cast them into the most remote corners, I will make them cease from human memory," for they are a nation devoid of counsel, and they have no understanding. Their vine is from the vine of Sodom and the fields of Gomorrah. Their grapes are grapes of gall; their clusters are bitter. Their wine is the venom of dragons and the cruel gall of poisonous snakes. All this is hidden with me, locked away in my treasuries. Vengeance and retribution belong to me. (Deuteronomy 32:20–35)

These words were spoken about that nation, and there are similar statements elsewhere, as in Isaiah 3:1, 2, 8; 5:3–6; Deuteronomy 9:5, 6; Matthew

12:39; 23:27, 28; John 8:44; and all through Jeremiah and Ezekiel. All the same, these statements that seem to contradict each other turn out to be in agreement in the light of a body of teaching, which tells us that Israel and Judah in the Word do not mean Israel and Judah but the church in each of two senses—one in which it lies in ruins and the other in which it is to be restored by the Lord. There are other contrasts like this in the Word that enable us to see that the Word cannot be understood apart from a body of teaching.

We can tell from all this that people who read the Word without a **52** body of teaching or who do not get themselves a body of teaching from the Word are in complete darkness about truth. Their minds are wandering and unstable, prone to error and liable to heresies. Such people will in fact embrace heresies if those heresies have gained any popularity or authority and their own reputation is therefore not in danger. For them the Word is like a lampstand without a lamp, and while they seem to be seeing a great many things in their darkness, they actually see practically nothing because a body of teaching is the only lamp. I have seen people like this examined by angels, and it was found that they can use the Word to justify whatever they choose; and the things they justify are those that appeal to their self-centeredness and their love for people who are on their side. I have also seen them stripped of their clothing, a sign of their lack of truths. In that world, truths are clothing.

2. *A body of teaching must be drawn from the literal meaning of the* **53** *Word and supported by it.* This is because there and only there the Lord is present with us, enlightening us and teaching us the truths of the church. Further, the Lord never does anything in a way that is less than complete, and it is in its literal meaning that the Word is in its fullness, as explained above [§§37–49]. That is why a body of teaching must be drawn from the literal meaning.

The reason the Word is not only understood but also shines with the **54** aid of a body of teaching is that the Word is not understandable apart from a body of teaching but is like a lampstand with no lamp, as just noted [§52]. So the Word understood by means of a body of teaching is like a lampstand with a burning lamp on it. We then see more than we had seen before and understand what we had not understood before. Things that are obscure and contradictory we either do not see and ignore or we see and explain in such a way that they harmonize with our body of teaching.

The experience of the Christian world bears witness to the fact that people see the Word through their body of teaching and explain it from that perspective. Obviously, all Protestants see the Word in the light of their teachings and explain it accordingly. Catholics too see it and explain it in the light of their teachings, and Jews see it and explain it in the light of theirs. A body of false teaching yields false beliefs, and a body of true teaching yields true beliefs. We can therefore see that a body of true teaching is like a light in the darkness and like signposts along the way.

However, our body of teaching must not only be drawn from the literal meaning of the Word, it must be supported by it as well, since if it is not supported by it, the truth of our body of teaching would seem to contain only our own intelligence and none of the Lord's divine wisdom. That would make our body of teaching a castle in the air and not on the ground, a castle with no foundation.

55 A body of teaching made up of genuine truth can actually be drawn entirely from the literal meaning of the Word because in that meaning the Word is like a clothed person whose hands and face are bare. Everything that has to do with how we live and therefore with our salvation is bare, while the rest is clothed; and in many places where the meaning is clothed it shows through like a face seen through a thin veil. As the truths of the Word are multiplied by being loved and in this way gain coherence, they shine through their clothing more and more clearly and become more visible. A body of teaching is the means to this too.

56 People may believe that a body of genuinely true teaching can be acquired by the use of the spiritual meaning of the Word, the meaning that comes through a knowledge of correspondences. This is not how we develop a body of teaching, though. It is only how we illustrate and reinforce it, since, as already noted in §26, no one gains access to spiritual meaning through correspondences without first being focused on genuine truths as a result of a body of teaching. People who are not first focused on genuine truths can distort the meaning of the Word by the use of a few familiar correspondences, connecting and interpreting them with a view to supporting whatever is lodged in their minds as a result of their preconceptions.

Not only that, the spiritual meaning is not granted to anyone unless it is granted by the Lord alone; and it is guarded by him the way he guards heaven, because heaven is within it. Priority, then, should be given to the study of the Word in its literal meaning. It is the only ground for a body of teaching.

57 3. *The genuine truth that a body of teaching should have can be seen in the literal meaning of the Word only when we are being enlightened by the*

Lord. Enlightenment comes only from the Lord and for people who love truths because they are true and who put them to use in their lives. For others, there is no enlightenment in the Word.

The reason enlightenment comes only from the Lord is that the Lord is present in every bit of the Word. The reason enlightenment happens for people who love truths because they are true and who put them to use in their lives is that they are in the Lord and the Lord is in them. In fact, the Lord is his divine truth. When divine truth is loved because it is divine truth (and it is loved when it is put to use), then the Lord is within it for us.

This is actually what the Lord is telling us in John:

> On that day you will know that you are in me and I am in you. The people who love me are those who have my commandments and do them; and I will love them and will manifest myself to them. I will come to them and make a home with them. (John 14:20, 21, 23)

And in Matthew:

> Blessed are the pure in heart, because they will see God. (Matthew 5:8)

These are the people who are in enlightenment when they read the Word, the people for whom the Word shines or glows.

The reason the Word shines or glows for them is that there is spiritual and heavenly meaning in the details of the Word, and these meanings are in heaven's light. So through these meanings and through their light the Lord flows into the earthly meaning and into its light for us. As a result, we recognize what is true because of an inner perception that enables us to see it in our thinking. This happens whenever we desire the truth because it is true. So this desire gives rise to perception and this perception gives rise to thought; the result is the acknowledgment we refer to as faith. **58**

I need to say more about this, though, in the next chapter, on the Lord's union with us through the Word [§§62–69].

The first task [of those who seek enlightenment when they read the Word] is to put together a body of teaching for themselves from the literal meaning of the Word. That is how they light a lamp in order to go further. Once they have put together a body of teaching and lit the lamp, they see the Word in the light of that lamp. **59**

However, people who have not put together a body of teaching for themselves first look to see whether the theological perspective offered by others and generally accepted does in fact agree with the Word; and they accept what agrees and dissent from what does not. That is how they form their body of teaching, and through their body of teaching, their faith.

This [enlightenment] happens, though, only for people who are able to contemplate things without being distracted by their professional responsibilities in this world. If they love truths because they are true and put them to use in their lives, they have enlightenment from the Lord, and other people whose lives are to any degree guided by truths can learn from them.

60 It is very different for us if we read the Word with a body of false religious teaching in our mind, and even more different if we use the Word to support those teachings and then focus on earthly wealth or our own glory. Then it is as though the truth of the Word were in the shadow of night and what is false were in the light of day. What we read is true, but we do not see it; and if we see even a shadow of the truth we distort it. We are then the people of whom the Lord said that they have eyes, but they do not see, and ears, but they do not understand (Matthew 13:14, 15). This is because nothing blinds us more completely than our self-importance and our convincing ourselves of what is false. Our self-importance is our infatuation with ourselves and our consequent pride in our intelligence; and our convincing ourselves of what is false is a darkness that pretends to be light. Our light in that case is entirely earthly, and our sight is like that of someone who sees ghosts in the dark.

61 I have been granted the opportunity to talk with any number of individuals after their death who had believed they were going to shine like stars in heaven because, they said, they had revered the Word, had read it through time and again, and had gained much from their reading that served to support the dogmas of their faith. All this led to their being celebrated as scholars, which in turn led them to believe they would become Michaels and Raphaels. [2] However, many of them were examined to find out what love had inspired their study of the Word, and it turned out that for some it was self-infatuation, a desire to look important in the eyes of the world and therefore be revered as leaders in the church, while for others it was worldliness and a desire for wealth. When they were asked what they had learned from the Word, it turned out that they knew nothing that was really true. All they knew was distorted truth, which is essentially false. They were told that this was because they themselves and the world were their goals—or were what they loved the most, which amounts to the same thing—and not the Lord and heaven. If ourselves and the world are our goals, then when we read the Word our minds are stuck on ourselves and the world. This means that our thinking is constantly focused on our self-importance, which is in darkness with respect to everything that has to do with heaven. People in this state cannot be lifted out of their self-infatuation by the Lord and thus raised up into heaven's light, so they are not open to any inflow from the Lord through heaven, either.

[3] I have seen them let into heaven, but when it was found that they were lacking in truths, they were expelled. Even so, they retained the prideful conviction that they were worthy.

It worked out otherwise for individuals who studied the Word from a desire to know what was true because it was true and because it could be put to use in their lives not only for their own benefit but for the benefit of their neighbor. I have seen them raised up into heaven and therefore into the light of divine truth there; and at the same time they have been lifted up into angelic wisdom and into its happiness, which is eternal life.

By Means of the Literal Meaning of the Word We Unite with the Lord and Form a Companionship with Angels

THE reason we have union with the Lord through the Word is that **62** the Word is entirely about him; and it is because of this that the Lord is its entire content and is called "the Word" [John 1:14], as was explained in *Teachings on the Lord* [§§1–2]. The reason the union takes place in the literal meaning is that this is where the Word is in its fullness, holiness, and power, as was explained previously under the appropriate heading [§§37–49]. This union is not something we can see, but it lies within our longing for what is true and our higher perception of it, so it lies within our inner love for and faith in divine truth.

The reason we have companionship with angels of heaven through **63** the literal meaning is that within the literal meaning there are spiritual and heavenly levels of meaning, and those levels are the ones on which angels are focused. Angels of the spiritual kingdom focus on the spiritual meaning of the Word and angels of the heavenly kingdom focus on the heavenly meaning. These meanings unfold from the earthly meaning of the Word, which is the literal meaning, when anyone who has become truly human is absorbed in it. The unfolding is instantaneous, so the companionship is as well.

64 Abundant experience has made it clear to me that spiritual angels are focused on the spiritual meaning of the Word and that heavenly angels are focused on its heavenly meaning. I have been made aware that when I was reading the Word in its literal meaning a communication was opened with one community or another of the heavens, and that spiritual angels were understanding in a spiritual way, and heavenly angels in a heavenly way, what I was understanding in an earthly way, and that this was happening instantaneously. I have been aware of this so many thousand times that I can no longer have any doubt about it.

[2] There are also spirits who live underneath the heavens who misuse this communication. What they do is repeat some things that are said in the literal meaning of the Word and promptly identify and mark the community with which communication has been effected. This too I have often seen and heard.

This kind of firsthand experience has taught me that the Word in its literal meaning is a divinely granted means of union with the Lord and with heaven. On this union by means of the Word, see also what is presented in *Heaven and Hell* 303–310.

65 I need to explain briefly how this unfolding of meanings happens, but in order to understand it, we need to go back to what was said earlier, in §§6 and 38, about sequential arrangement and simultaneous arrangement—namely, that what is heavenly, what is spiritual, and what is earthly follow each other in sequence from the highest things that are in heaven to those things most remote from them in this world, and that in a simultaneous arrangement the same realities are within the most remote, which is the earthly, side by side from the innermost to the outermost. It was also explained [§38] that by the same token, the sequential meanings of the Word—the heavenly and the spiritual—are simultaneously present in the earthly meaning.

Once we grasp this, we can begin to understand how the two meanings, the spiritual and the heavenly, are unfolded from the earthly meaning when we are reading the Word. A spiritual angel will call to mind something spiritual and a heavenly angel will call to mind something heavenly.

They cannot do otherwise: the meanings have qualities that are similar in type and are in harmony with the angels' nature and essence.

First, though, let me illustrate this with comparisons from the three kingdoms of nature, which we refer to as the animal, plant, and mineral kingdoms. **66**

From *the animal kingdom:* From food, once it has been digested, the blood vessels derive and call forth their blood, the nerve fibers their juice, and the substances that are the sources of the fibers the fine fluid of the soul.

From *the plant kingdom:* A tree, with its trunk, branches, leaves, and fruit, is based on its roots, and through its roots draws and calls forth from the ground a coarser sap for the trunk, branches, and leaves, a finer sap for the flesh of its fruit, and the finest for the seeds within the fruit.

From *the mineral kingdom:* At various locations deep within the earth there are deposits of ore pregnant with gold, silver, and iron. From the hidden gases exhaled by the earth, the gold, silver, and iron each draw their own basic substance.

Now I may offer some examples to make clear how spiritual angels draw their meaning, and heavenly angels their meaning, from the earthly meaning that the Word presents to us. We may take five of the Ten Commandments as examples. **67**

The commandment *"Honor your father and your mother"* [Exodus 20:12; Deuteronomy 5:16]. We understand "father and mother" to mean our earthly fathers and mothers and any individuals who act as fathers and mothers for us. We understand honoring them to mean admiring them and being obedient to them. A spiritual angel, though, understands "father" to mean the Lord and "mother" to mean the church; and they understand honoring to mean loving. But a heavenly angel understands "father" to mean the Lord's divine love and "mother" the Lord's divine wisdom, and honoring to mean doing what is good because of him.

[2] The commandment *"You are not to steal"* [Exodus 20:15; Deuteronomy 5:19]. We understand stealing to mean theft, cheating, or depriving others of their assets by any means. A spiritual angel understands stealing to mean using false and evil devices to deprive people of the truths of their faith and their good, caring actions. A heavenly angel, though, understands stealing to mean giving ourselves credit for what belongs to the Lord and claiming his righteousness and worth as our own.

[3] The commandment *"You are not to commit adultery"* [Exodus 20:14; Deuteronomy 5:18]. We understand committing adultery to mean the act of adultery, as well as promiscuity, indecent behavior, filthy language, and impure thoughts. A spiritual angel understands adultery to

mean perverting what is good in the Word and falsifying its truths. A heavenly angel, though, understands adultery to mean denying the divine nature of the Lord and profaning the Word.

[4] The commandment *"You are not to kill"* [Exodus 20:13; Deuteronomy 5:17]. We understand killing to mean harboring hatred as well [Matthew 5:22] and seeking revenge even as far as killing. A spiritual angel understands killing to mean playing the role of a devil and killing someone's soul [Matthew 10:28; Luke 12:5]. A heavenly angel, though, understands killing to mean hating the Lord and hating anything that belongs to the Lord.

[5] The commandment *"You are not to bear false witness"* [Exodus 20:16; Deuteronomy 5:20]. We understand bearing false witness to mean lying and slandering people as well. A spiritual angel understands bearing false witness to mean saying and persuading others to believe that something false is true and that something evil is good, and the reverse. A heavenly angel, though, understands bearing false witness to mean blasphemy against the Lord and the Word.

[6] This enables us to see how spiritual and heavenly meanings are unfolded and drawn from the earthly meaning of the Word that contains them; and strange as it may seem, angels draw these meanings out without knowing what we are thinking. Nevertheless, angels' thinking and our thinking become one because of correspondences, just as a goal, its means, and its results become one. Functionally, the goals are in the heavenly kingdom, the means in the spiritual kingdom, and the results in the earthly kingdom. This kind of union by correspondence comes from creation, and this is how we now associate with angels through the Word.

68 Another reason our companionship with angels is established through the earthly or literal meaning of the Word is that by virtue of our creation each of us has three levels of life—heavenly, spiritual, and earthly. As long as we are in this world we are focused on the earthly level, then on the spiritual level to the extent that we are intent on genuine truths, and then on the heavenly level to the extent that we are devoted to living by these truths. We do not, however, gain full access to that spiritual or heavenly level until after death. But there is more on this elsewhere.

69 Since it is through the Word that we unite with the Lord and form a companionship with angels, we may conclude that the Word alone contains spirit and life, just as the Lord said:

The words that I speak to you are spirit and are life. (John 6:63)

The water that I will give you will become a fountain of water, springing up into eternal life. (John 4:14)

Humankind does not live from bread alone but from every word that proceeds from the mouth of God. (Matthew 4:4)

Work for the food that endures to eternal life, which the Son of Humanity will give you. (John 6:27)

The Word Is in All the Heavens and Is the Source of Angelic Wisdom

UNTIL the present time, people have not known that the Word exists in heaven, and they could not know this as long as the church did not realize that angels and spirits are people just as we are in this world—like us in every respect except for the fact that they are spiritual and that everything around them has a spiritual origin, while we are earthly and everything around us has an earthly origin. As long as this lay hidden there was no way to know that there was a Word in heaven as well and that it was read both by angels there and by spirits who live underneath the heavens.

But to keep this from remaining hidden forever, I have been granted companionship with angels and spirits, to talk with them, to see what their circumstances are like, and then to report many things that I have heard and seen. This reporting was done in the book *Heaven and Hell* (published in London in 1758). That will enable you to see that angels and spirits are people and that they are abundantly supplied with everything we have in this world.

On angels and spirits being people, see §§73–77 and 453–456 of that work. On their circumstances being similar to ours in this world, see §§170–190. On their also having worship of God and preaching in churches, see §§221–227. On their having written materials and books, see §§258–264; and on the Word, see §259.

71 As for the Word in heaven, it is written in a spiritual style that is completely different from an earthly style. This spiritual style of writing consists entirely of letters that have individual meanings. There are also marks over the letters that heighten the meaning.

For angels of the spiritual kingdom the letters look like typeset letters in our world; and the letters for angels of the heavenly kingdom—each of which enfolds a whole meaning—are like the ancient Hebrew letters, variously curved, with marks over and within them.

[2] Since this is what their writing is like, there are no personal or place names in their Word as there are in ours. Instead of the names there are the realities that they mean. Instead of Moses, for example, the text reads "the historical books of the Word"; for Elijah, "the prophetic books"; for Abraham, Isaac, and Jacob, "the Lord in respect to his divine nature and his divine-human nature"; for Aaron, "priesthood" and for David, "monarchy," both in reference to the Lord; for the names of the twelve sons of Jacob or the tribes of Israel, various aspects of heaven and the church, and the same for the names of the Lord's twelve disciples; for Zion and Jerusalem, the church in respect to the Word and its body of teaching drawn from the Word; for the land of Canaan, the church itself; for the cities on either side of the Jordan, various elements of the church and its teachings; and so on and so forth.

It is the same with numbers. These are not found in the Word that is in heaven either, but instead there are the realities to which the numbers in our Word correspond.

We can therefore conclude that the Word in heaven is a Word that corresponds to our Word and that because of this they are one, for correspondences make unity.

72 It is wondrous that the Word in the heavens is written in such a way that ordinary people understand it simply and wise people understand it wisely. There are many marks and points over the letters that heighten the meaning, as already noted. Ordinary people pay no attention to these and do not know what they mean. The wise do pay attention to them, depending on how wise they are, even to the very wisest.

In every major community in heaven there is a copy of the Word that is written by angels inspired by the Lord, kept in that community's repository so that not a single point in it will be altered anywhere.

Our own Word is actually written like the Word in heaven, so that ordinary people understand it simply and wise people wisely, but this is accomplished in a different way.

The angels themselves confess that they get all their wisdom through **73** the Word, since the amount of light they enjoy depends on how focused they are on understanding the Word. Heaven's light is divine wisdom, which is light to their eyes.

In the repository where their copy of the Word is kept, the light is flaming and brilliant, surpassing every level of light found outside it in heaven. The reason is the one already stated [§§57, 62]—the Lord is in the Word.

The wisdom of heavenly angels surpasses that of spiritual angels by **74** almost as much as the wisdom of spiritual angels surpasses ours. This is because heavenly angels are focused on good, loving actions that come from the Lord, while spiritual angels are focused on truths of wisdom that come from the Lord. Wherever we find good actions that come from love, wisdom is dwelling with them. There is wisdom wherever we find truths, too, but only in an amount proportional to the presence of good actions that come from love. This is why the Word in the heavenly kingdom is written differently from the Word in the spiritual kingdom. In the version of the Word in the heavenly kingdom the letters themselves express good actions from love and the marks around them convey emotions; in the version of the Word in the spiritual kingdom the letters express truths that lead to wisdom and the marks convey insights.

We can tell from this what kind of wisdom lies hidden in the Word **75** we have in this world. Within it lies all angelic wisdom, which is inexpressible. It is in fact the container of that wisdom; and we become conscious of that wisdom after death if we have been made angels by the Lord through the Word.

The Existence of the Church Rests on the Word, and Its Quality Depends on the Quality of Its Understanding of the Word

THERE can be no doubt that the existence of the church rests on the **76** Word, since the Word is divine truth itself (§§1–4), the teachings of the church come from the Word (§§50–61), and our union with the Lord comes through the Word (§§62–69). However, some may doubt that our understanding of the Word is what makes the church, if only because there are people who believe that they are part of the church solely by virtue of having the Word, reading it, or hearing it from the pulpit, and by thus having acquired some knowledge of its literal meaning. They do not know how to understand a single thing in the Word, though, and some of them do not even attach much importance to the Word at all. So at this point I need to show that it is not the Word that makes the church but the way the Word is understood, and that the quality of the church depends on the quality of the understanding of the Word among the people who are in the church. This is shown by the following.

77   Whether or not the Word is the Word depends on our comprehension of it—that is, on how we understand it. If we do not understand it, we may of course call it "the Word," but for us it is not the Word.

The Word is truth depending on how it is understood, for the Word can be nontruth—it can be distorted. The Word is spirit and life depending on how we understand it, for the letter is dead if it is not understood.

Since we gain truth and life depending on how we understand the Word, we also gain faith and love depending on how we understand it, because faith has to do with truth and life has to do with love.

Since the church exists by means of its faith and love and is only as good as its faith and love, it follows that a church exists by means of its understanding of the Word and is only as good as its understanding of the Word. A church is worthy if it is focused on genuine truths, unworthy if it is not focused on genuine truths, and ruined if it is focused on distorted truths.

78   To continue, the Lord is present with us and united to us through the Word because the Lord is the Word and is virtually talking with us in it. There is also the fact that the Lord is divine truth itself, and that is what the Word is.

We can see from this that the extent to which we understand the Word determines the extent to which the Lord is present with us and at the same time united to us. This is because our understanding of the Word determines the truth we possess, as well as the faith that arises from that truth. Similarly, our understanding of the Word determines the love we have, as well as the way in which we live, which arises from that love. The Lord is present with us when we read the Word; but he is united to us only when we understand what is true from the Word and only in proportion to that understanding; and to the extent that the Lord is united to us the church is within us.

And the church is indeed something within us. The church that is outside us is the church of the many who have the church within them. This is the meaning of what the Lord said to the Pharisees when they asked him when the kingdom of God was coming—"The kingdom of God is within you" (Luke 17:21). Here the kingdom of God means the Lord, and the church from him.

There are many passages in the prophets about our understanding of the Word, passages about the church, where it tells us that the church exists only where the Word is properly understood, and that the quality of a church depends on the quality of the understanding of the Word among its members. There are also many passages in the prophets that describe the church among the Israelite and Jewish people, a church that was utterly destroyed and annihilated by the distortion of the Word's meaning or message, for this is exactly what destroys a church.

[2] The name Ephraim in the prophets, especially in Hosea, symbolizes both true and false understandings of the Word, because Ephraim in the Word means the understanding of the Word in the church. It is because the understanding of the Word makes a church that Ephraim is called "a precious child, and one born of delights" (Jeremiah 31:20), "the firstborn" (Jeremiah 31:9), "the strength of Jehovah's head" (Psalms 60:7; 108:8), "powerful" (Zechariah 10:7), and "filling a bow" (Zechariah 9:13); and the children of Ephraim are called "armed" and "bow shooters" (Psalms 78:9). The bow means a body of teaching from the Word fighting against what is false.

So too, Ephraim was transferred to the right of Israel and blessed, and accepted in place of Reuben (Genesis 48:5, 11, and following; [1 Chronicles 5:1]). And therefore Ephraim, together with his brother Manasseh, was exalted over all by Moses in his blessing of the children of Israel in the name of their father Joseph (Deuteronomy 33:13–17).

[3] The prophets, especially Hosea, also use "Ephraim" to describe what the church is like when its understanding of the Word has been lost, as we can see from the following:

> Israel and Ephraim will stumble. Ephraim will be desolate. Ephraim is oppressed and broken in judgment. I will be like a lion to Ephraim: I will tear them and leave; I will carry them off and no one will rescue them. (Hosea 5:5, 9, 11, 14)

79

What shall I do to you, Ephraim? Your holiness goes away like a cloud at dawn and like the morning dew that falls. (Hosea 6:4)

[4] They will not dwell in the land of Jehovah: Ephraim will go back to Egypt and will eat what is unclean in Assyria. (Hosea 9:3)

The land of Jehovah is the church, Egypt is the preoccupation of the earthly self with mere facts, and Assyria is rationalizing based on those facts; all of which lead to distortion of the Word in regard to the way it is understood. That is why it says that Ephraim will go back to Egypt and will eat what is unclean in Assyria.

[5] Ephraim feeds on the wind and chases the east wind. Every day he increases lies and devastation. He makes a covenant with Assyria, and oil is carried down into Egypt. (Hosea 12:1)

To feed on the wind, chase the east wind, and increase lies and devastation is to distort what is true and in this way destroy the church.

[6] Much the same is also meant by Ephraim's whoredom, since whoredom means distortion of the way the Word is understood—that is, distortion of its genuine truth. See the following passages:

I know Ephraim; he has committed whoredom in every way and Israel has been defiled. (Hosea 5:3)

I have seen something foul in the house of Israel: Ephraim has committed whoredom there, and Israel has been defiled. (Hosea 6:10)

Israel is the church itself and Ephraim is the understanding of the Word that is the source of the church and that determines its quality, so it says that Ephraim has committed whoredom and Israel has been defiled.

[7] Since the church among Jews had been completely destroyed because of its distortions, it says of Ephraim,

Am I to give you up, Ephraim? Am I to hand you over, Israel? Like Admah? Shall I make you like Zeboiim? (Hosea 11:8)

Since the book of the prophet Hosea, from the first chapter to the last, is about the distortion of the Word and the consequent destruction of the church, and since whoredom means the distortion of truth in the church, the prophet was commanded to represent that state of the church by taking a whore as his wife and fathering children by her (chapter 1); and also by forming a relationship with a woman who was committing adultery (chapter 3).

[8] These instances have been presented so that readers may know and be assured from the Word that the quality of a church depends on the quality of the understanding of the Word in it—outstanding and priceless if its understanding comes from genuine truths from the Word, but in ruins, actually filthy, if it comes from distortions.

For further evidence that Ephraim means the understanding of the Word, and in its opposite sense a distorted understanding leading to the destruction of the church, you may check some other passages that deal with Ephraim: Hosea 4:17, 18; 7:1, 11; 8:9, 11; 9:11, 12, 13, 16; 10:11; 11:3; 12:1, 8, 14; 13:1, 8, 14; Isaiah 17:3; 28:1; Jeremiah 4:15; 31:6, 18; 50:19; Ezekiel 37:16; 48:5; Obadiah verse 19; Zechariah 9:10.

There Is a Marriage of the Lord and the Church in the Details of the Word and a Consequent Marriage of Goodness and Truth

UNTIL the present time, no one has seen that there is a marriage of the Lord and the church in the details of the Word and a consequent marriage of goodness and truth, and no one could see it because the spiritual meaning of the Word had not been uncovered, and without this, the marriage cannot be seen. **80**

There are two levels of meaning in the Word that are hidden within the literal meaning, namely, a spiritual level and a heavenly level. Spiritually understood, the contents of the Word refer for the most part to the church, while understood on a heavenly level they refer for the most part to the Lord. On a spiritual level they also refer to divine truth and on a heavenly level they refer to divine goodness. As a result, this marriage is found in the literal meaning of the Word.

However, this is not apparent to anyone who does not know the meanings of words and names on the basis of the spiritual and heavenly meanings of the Word, since some words and names focus attention on what is good and some on what is true, and some include both, so unless this is realized the marriage in the details of the Word cannot be seen. That is why this mystery has not been disclosed before.

81 Because this marriage is in the details of the Word, time and again there are paired expressions in the Word that seem to be saying the same thing twice. However, they are not mere repetitions. One focuses on what is good and the other on what is true, and their combination makes a union of the two and therefore a single thing. That is actually the basis of the divinity of the Word and of its holiness, since in every divine work goodness is united to truth and truth is united to goodness.

82 I have said that there is a marriage of the Lord and the church in the details of the Word and a *consequent* marriage of goodness and truth because wherever there is a marriage of the Lord and the church there is also a marriage of goodness and truth. The latter comes from the former because when the church or its membership is focused on what is true, the Lord flows into their truths with what is good and brings those truths to life. Or to put it another way, when the church or members of the church are intelligent because of truths, then the Lord flows into their intelligence through the good they do out of love and caring, and fills their intelligence with life.

83 Each of us has two faculties of life, called understanding and will. Our understanding receives what is true and therefore receives what is wise, and our will receives what is good and therefore receives love. These must become one if we are to be part of the church; and they do become one when we form our understanding from genuine truth, to all appearances doing this ourselves, and when our will is filled with a love for doing good, which is accomplished by the Lord. In this way we have a life of what is true and a life of what is good, the life of what is true in our understanding from our will and the life of what is good in our will by means of our understanding; and this is a marriage of truth and goodness for us and a marriage of the Lord and the church for us.

But there is more on this mutual union, here called a marriage, in *Angelic Wisdom about Divine Providence, [Angelic Wisdom] about Divine Love and Wisdom,* and *[Angelic Wisdom] about Life.*

84 It can seem to readers who pay attention to such things that there are paired expressions in the Word that seem to be repetitions of the same thing—brother [and companion], for example, [poor] and needy, waste and desolation, emptiness and void, enemy and foe, sin and iniquity, wrath and rage, nation and people, joy and gladness, grief and tears, justice and judgment, and the like. They do seem to be synonyms, but they are not, since brother, poor, waste, [emptiness,] enemy, sin, wrath, nation, joy, grief, and justice describe what is good (or in an opposite sense, what is evil), while companion, needy, desolation, void, foe, iniquity, rage, people, gladness, tears, and judgment describe what is true (or in an opposite sense, what is false). It seems to a reader who is unfamiliar with this mystery that poor and needy, waste and desolation, emptiness and void, enemy and foe are the same thing, as are sin and iniquity, wrath and rage, nation and people, joy and gladness, grief and tears, justice and judgment; yet they are not the same thing. Rather they become one thing by being brought together.

[2] Many other things are paired in the Word, like fire and flame, gold and silver, bronze and iron, wood and stone, bread and water, bread and wine, purple and linen, and so on, and this is because fire, gold, bronze, wood, bread, and purple mean something good, while flame, silver, iron, stone, water, wine, and linen mean something true. In the same vein, it says that we are to love God with our whole heart and our whole soul and that God is going to create in us a new heart and a new spirit, "heart" describing the good that comes from love and "soul" the truth that comes from that good.

There are also expressions that occur alone with nothing appended because they designate both goodness and truth. These and many other expressions, though, are evident only to angels and to people who are aware of the spiritual meaning even while they are focused on the earthly meaning.

It would be a waste of time to show from the Word that there are in the Word paired expressions like these that seem like repetitions of the same thing, because that would fill many pages. To banish doubt, though, I would like to cite some passages where *judgment* and *justice* occur together, then *nation* and *people,* and then *joy* and *gladness.*

The following are passages where *judgment* and *justice* are paired:

The city used to be full of [good] *judgment; justice* used to spend its nights there. (Isaiah 1:21)

Zion will be redeemed in *justice,* and those of her who are brought back, in *judgment.* (Isaiah 1:27)

Jehovah Sabaoth will be exalted in *judgment,* and God, the Holy One, will be hallowed in *justice.* (Isaiah 5:16)

He will sit upon the throne of David and over his kingdom, to establish it in *judgment* and in *justice*. (Isaiah 9:7)

Let Jehovah be exalted, because he dwells on high and has filled the earth with *judgment* and *justice*. (Isaiah 33:5)

Jehovah says, "Watch over *judgment* and perform *justice,* for my *salvation* is at hand so that my *justice* may be revealed." (Isaiah 56:1)

As though they were a nation that did *justice* and had not abandoned the *judgment* of their God, they would ask for *judgments of justice*. (Isaiah 58:2)

Swear by the living Jehovah in *judgment* and in *justice*. (Jeremiah 4:2)

The one who glories should glory in this, that Jehovah is bringing about *judgment* and *justice* on the earth. (Jeremiah 9:24)

Do *judgment* and *justice*. Woe to those who build their house without *justice* and their upper chambers without *judgment.* Has not your father done *judgment* and *justice?* Then it will be well for him. (Jeremiah 22:3, 13, 15)

I will raise up for David a righteous branch who will rule as king and bring about *judgment* and *justice* on earth. (Jeremiah 23:5; 33:15)

If a man is righteous and has practiced *judgment* and *justice* . . . (Ezekiel 18:5)

If the ungodly turn back and practice *judgment* and *justice,* [their former deeds] will not be remembered against them. They have practiced *judgment* and *justice;* they will surely live. (Ezekiel 33:14, 16)

I will betroth myself to you forever in *justice* and *judgment,* and in *mercy* and *compassion*. (Hosea 2:19)

Let *judgment* flow down like water, and *justice* like a mighty torrent. (Amos 5:24)

You have turned *judgment* into gall and the fruit of *justice* into wormwood. (Amos 6:12)

Jehovah will plead my case and bring about a *judgment* for me. He will lead me into the light, and I will see his *justice*. (Micah 7:9)

Jehovah, your *justice* is like the mountains of God; your *judgments* are a great deep. (Psalms 36:6)

Jehovah will bring forth his *justice* like light and *judgment* like noonday. (Psalms 37:6)

Jehovah will judge his people with *justice* and his needy ones with *judgment*. (Psalms 72:2)

Justice and *judgment* are the foundation of your throne. (Psalms 89:14)

. . . when I will have learned the *judgments* of your *justice*. Seven times a day I praise you for the *judgments* of your *justice*. (Psalms 119:7, 164)

Gad enacts the *justice* of Jehovah and his *judgment* with Israel. (Deuteronomy 33:21)

The Spirit of Truth will convict the world concerning *justice* and *judgment*. (John 16:8, 10)

There are other such passages as well.

The reason judgment and justice are mentioned so often is that the Word says "judgment" in reference to what is true and "justice" in reference to what is good; so "doing judgment and justice" also means acting on the basis of what is true and on the basis of what is good.

The reason the Word says "judgment" in reference to what is true and "justice" in reference to what is good is that the Lord's government in the spiritual kingdom is called "judgment," while the Lord's government in the heavenly kingdom is called "justice" (see *Heaven and Hell* 214–215). Because the Word says "judgment" in reference to what is true, in some passages it speaks of *truth* and *justice,* as in Isaiah 11:5, Psalms 85:11, and elsewhere.

We can see more clearly from passages where it says *nations and peoples* that there are in the Word repetitions of what seems to be the same thing for the sake of the marriage of goodness and truth. See, for example, the following passages: **86**

Woe to a sinful *nation,* to a *people* weighed down with iniquity. (Isaiah 1:4)

The *peoples* walking in darkness have seen a great light; you have multiplied the *nation*. (Isaiah 9:2, 3)

Assyria is the rod of my anger. I will send him against a hypocritical *nation;* I will appoint him against the *people* of my rage. (Isaiah 10:5, 6)

It will happen on that day that the *nations* will seek the root of Jesse, the one who stands as a sign for the *peoples*. (Isaiah 11:10)

Jehovah is striking the *peoples* with a plague that cannot be healed and ruling the *nations* in anger. (Isaiah 14:6)

On that day a gift will be brought to Jehovah Sabaoth—a *people* scattered and shaven and a *nation* measured and trampled. (Isaiah 18:7)

A strong *people* will honor you; a city of powerful *nations* will fear you. (Isaiah 25:3)

Jehovah will swallow up the covering that is over all *peoples* and the veil that is over all *nations*. (Isaiah 25:7)

Come near, O *nations,* and listen, O *peoples.* (Isaiah 34:1)

I have called you to be a covenant for the *people,* a light for the *nations.* (Isaiah 42:6)

Let all the *nations* be gathered together, and let the *peoples* convene. (Isaiah 43:9)

Behold, I will lift up my hand toward the *nations,* and my sign toward the *peoples.* (Isaiah 49:22)

I have made him a witness to the *peoples,* a prince and a lawgiver to the *nations.* (Isaiah 55:4, 5)

Behold, a *people* is coming from the land of the north and a great *nation* from the farthest parts of the earth. (Jeremiah 6:22)

I will no longer let you hear the slander of the *nations,* and you will not bear the reproach of the *peoples* anymore. (Ezekiel 36:15)

All *peoples* and *nations* will worship him. (Daniel 7:14)

Do not allow the *nations* to turn [your heritage] into a joke or to say among the *peoples,* "Where is their God?" (Joel 2:17)

The remnant of my *people* will plunder them and the remainder of my *nation* will possess them. (Zephaniah 2:9)

Many *peoples* and vast *nations* will come to seek Jehovah Sabaoth in Jerusalem. (Zechariah 8:22)

My eyes have seen your salvation, which you have prepared before the face of all *peoples,* a light to bring revelation to the *nations.* (Luke 2:30, 31, 32)

You have redeemed us by your blood out of every *people* and *nation.* (Revelation 5:9)

You must prophesy again about *peoples* and *nations.* (Revelation 10:11)

You will make me the head of the *nations; people* I have not known will serve me. (Psalms 18:43)

Jehovah makes the counsel of the *nations* ineffective; he overturns the thoughts of the *peoples.* (Psalms 33:10)

You are making us a byword among the *nations,* a shaking of the head among the *peoples.* (Psalms 44:14)

Jehovah will subdue *peoples* under us and *nations* under our feet. Jehovah has ruled over the *nations;* those who are willing among the *peoples* have gathered. (Psalms 47:3, 8, 9)

The *peoples* will praise you, the *nations* will be glad and rejoice, because you are going to judge the *peoples* with righteousness and lead the *nations* in the land. (Psalms 67:3, 4)

Remember me, Jehovah, in the good pleasure of your *people,* so that I may be glad in the joy of your *nations.* (Psalms 106:4, 5)

There are other passages as well.

The reason it says both nations and peoples is that "nations" means people who are focused on what is good (and in an opposite sense, on what is evil) and "peoples" means those who are focused on what is true (and in an opposite sense, on what is false). That is why those who are in the Lord's spiritual kingdom are called peoples, while those in the Lord's heavenly kingdom are called nations. The underlying reason is that everyone in the spiritual kingdom is focused on what is true and therefore on wisdom, while everyone in the heavenly kingdom is focused on what is good and therefore on love.

It is much the same in the other instances—for example, where it says *joy* it also says *gladness,* as in the following examples.

87

Behold *joy* and *gladness,* [people] slaughtering an ox. (Isaiah 22:13)

They will obtain *joy* and *gladness;* sadness and groaning will flee. (Isaiah 35:10; 51:11)

Gladness and *joy* have been cut off from the house of our God. (Joel 1:16)

There will be an end to the voice of *joy* and the voice of *gladness*. (Jeremiah 7:34; 25:10)

The fast of the tenth month will become *joy* and *gladness* for the house of Judah. (Zechariah 8:19)

So that we may *rejoice* all our days, make us *glad*. (Psalms 90:14, 15)

Be *glad* in Jerusalem; *rejoice* in her. (Isaiah 66:10)

Rejoice and be *glad,* O daughter of Edom. (Lamentations 4:21)

Let the heavens be *glad* and the earth *rejoice*. (Psalms 96:11)

They will make me hear *joy* and *gladness*. (Psalms 51:8)

Joy and *gladness* will be found in Zion, praise and the voice of song. (Isaiah 51:3)

You will have *gladness,* and many will *rejoice* over his birth. (Luke 1:14)

I will make the voice of *joy* and the voice of *gladness* cease, the voice of the bridegroom and the voice of the bride. (Jeremiah 7:34; 16:9; 25:10)

Once again the voice of *joy* and the voice of *gladness* will be heard in this place, and the voice of the bridegroom and the voice of the bride. (Jeremiah 33:10, 11)

There are other passages as well.

[2] The reason it says both "joy" and "gladness" is that joy has to do with what is good and gladness with what is true, or joy has to do with love and gladness with wisdom. The underlying cause is that joy is of the heart and gladness is of the spirit, or joy arises from our will and gladness from our understanding.

We can see that this also involves a marriage of the Lord and the church from the fact that it speaks of "the voice of joy and the voice of gladness, the voice of the bridegroom and the voice of the bride" (Jeremiah 7:34; 16:9; 25:10; 33:10, 11), and the Lord is the bridegroom and the church is the bride. On the Lord as the bridegroom, see Matthew 9:15; Mark 2:19, 20; Luke 5:34, 35; and on the church as the bride, see Revelation 21:2, 9; 22:17. That is why John the Baptist said, "The bridegroom is the one who has the bride" (John 3:29).

88 Because of the marriage of the Lord with the church in the details of the Word (or because of the marriage of divine goodness and divine truth, which is the same thing), in many passages it says "Jehovah" and

"God," and "Jehovah" and "the Holy One of Israel" as though they were two when in fact they are one. In fact, "Jehovah" means the Lord with respect to his divine goodness and "God" [and "the Holy One of Israel"] mean the Lord with respect to his divine truth. See *Teachings on the Lord* 34, 38, and 46 for many occurrences in the Word of "Jehovah" and "God" and of "Jehovah" and "the Holy One of Israel" when the intent is to communicate that the two are one, who is the Lord.

Since there is a marriage of the Lord and the church throughout the Word, we can be quite sure that absolutely everything in the Word is about the Lord, as I undertook to show in §§1–7 of *Teachings on the Lord.* The church, which is also the subject, is the Lord as well, since the Lord teaches that members of the church are in him and that he is in them (John 6:56; 14:20, 21; 15:5, 7).

Since we are dealing here with the divinity and holiness of the Word, I may add an interesting story to what has just been said.

On one occasion a little sheet of paper was sent down to me from heaven. It was inscribed with Hebrew letters, but written in the way the ancients used to write. Letters that today are largely straight were curved then and had little tips that turned upward. Angels who were with me at the time said that they found complete meanings in the letters themselves. They derived these meanings especially from the curvature of the lines and of the tips of the letters. They went on to explain what the letters meant individually and in combination, saying the *h* that was added to the names of Abram and Sarai [Genesis 17:5, 15] meant what was infinite and eternal. They also explained to me the meaning of the Word in Psalms 32:2 on the basis of the letters alone. Taken all together, the meaning of the letters was that *the Lord is also compassionate to people who do evil.*

[2] The angels told me that the writing in the third heaven consists of letters that are bent and curved in various ways, each of which has a specific meaning. The vowels in that writing indicate sounds that correspond to the feelings expressed. Angels in that heaven cannot pronounce the vowel sounds of *i* and *e,* so instead they use *y* and *eu.* The vowel sounds of *a, o,* and *u* are in common use among them because these give a full sound. They also said that they do not pronounce any consonants as hard, they only pronounce them as soft, which is why some Hebrew letters have dots in them to signal that they are to be pronounced [as hard, but no dots when they are to be pronounced] as soft. The angels said that [pronouncing] these letters as hard was a practice in the spiritual

heaven because there they are focused on what is true, and truth is open to what is hard. The goodness that is the focus of angels of the heavenly kingdom, or the third heaven, is not open to what is hard.

The angels [with me] said that the written Word they have also has curved letters with little tips or strokes that add to the meaning. I could see from this the meaning of the Lord's words,

> Not one little letter or the tip of one letter will pass from the law until all of it is fulfilled. (Matthew 5:18)

and

> It is easier for heaven and earth to pass away than for the tip of one letter of the law to fall. (Luke 16:17)

It Is Possible to Wrench Heretical Ideas from the Literal Meaning of the Word, but What Is Damning Is to Convince Ourselves [That They Are True]

91 I have already shown [§§51–52] that the Word cannot be understood apart from a body of teaching and that a body of teaching serves as a kind of lamp that enables us to see genuine truths. This is because the Word is composed entirely of correspondences, which is why there are so many semblances of truth in it that are not bare truths, as well as many things written for the comprehension of earthly, sense-oriented people. Even so, they have been written so that ordinary people can understand them simply, intelligent people intelligently, and wise people wisely.

Now, since that is what the Word is like, semblances of truth—clothed truths—can be seized on as bare truths, which become false if we convince ourselves of them. This is done by people who believe they are wiser than others, though in fact they are not wise at all. Wisdom is seeing whether something is true before convincing ourselves of it, not convincing ourselves of whatever happens to suit us. This latter is what people do when they are particularly good at proving things and have pride in their own intelligence. The former, though, is what people do who love truths and are moved by them because they are true and who put them to use in their lives. These people are enlightened by the Lord and see truths in the light of truths. The others are enlightened by themselves and see falsities in the light of what is false.

We can tell that semblances of truth, which are clothed truths, can be taken from the Word as bare truths and that they become false when we convince ourselves of them, if we think of the abundance of heresies that have existed and still exist in Christianity. **92**

The heretical ideas themselves do not hurt us. What hurts us is living evil lives, and also using the Word and the rationalizations of our earthly self to convince ourselves of the false notions inherent in the heretical ideas.

We are all born into the religion of our parents and are introduced into it in early childhood, and we remain in it afterward, unable to extricate ourselves from its falsities because we are preoccupied with our dealings with this world. Living evil lives, though, and convincing ourselves of false beliefs even to the point of destroying genuine truth—that does condemn us. If we stay with our religion and believe in God (and within the Christian faith that means we believe in the Lord and revere the Word) and we live by the principles of the Ten Commandments out of religious conviction, we will not swear allegiance to notions that are false. Therefore when we hear something true and perceive it in our own particular way, we are in a position to embrace it and be led out of our former false beliefs. However, this will not happen if we have thoroughly convinced ourselves of the falsities of our religion, because once we have convinced ourselves of something false, that belief is there to stay and cannot be uprooted. Once we have convinced ourselves of something false we have in effect sworn allegiance to it, especially if it appeals to our beloved self-importance and therefore to our pride in our own wisdom.

I have talked with individuals in the spiritual world who lived some centuries ago and who had convinced themselves of the falsities of their religion, and I have found them to be still firmly loyal to the same opinions. I have talked with some there who were of the same religion and who thought along the same lines but had not inwardly convinced themselves of those falsities, and I have found that when given angelic instruction **93** they rejected their false beliefs and absorbed true ones. These latter were saved while the others were not.

Everyone is given angelic instruction after death, and we are accepted if we see what is true and see what is false on the basis of what is true, because after death everyone is given the ability to see truths spiritually. The people who do see what is true are the ones who have not convinced themselves [of what is false]; but the ones who have convinced themselves [of what is false] do not want to see what is true. If they do see it they turn their backs to it and either ridicule it or distort it.

94 Let me offer an example by way of illustration. There are many passages in the Word where the Lord is described as wrathful, raging, vengeful, and is said to punish, cast into hell, tempt, and the like. People who believe this in simplicity and therefore fear God and take care not to sin against him are not condemned because of their simplistic faith. However, if people convince themselves that these descriptions of the Lord are true even to the point of actually believing that wrath, rage, vengefulness, and the like, which are evil, are real characteristics of the Lord and that he does punish us and does cast us into hell out of wrath, rage, and vengefulness, they are condemned because they have destroyed the real truth, which is that the Lord is love itself, mercy itself, and goodness itself, and anyone who is these qualities is incapable of wrath, rage, and vengeance. Attributing the other qualities to the Lord is based on the way things seem. The same principle applies in many other cases.

95 There is an example from the physical world that may serve to illustrate the fact that within the literal sense are many semblances of truth that have genuine truth hidden within them, and that it does us no harm to think and talk as though they were true but that it does do us harm to convince ourselves of them to the point of destroying the genuine truth hidden within. I offer this example because something down to earth is more clearly instructive and persuasive than something spiritual.

[2] To all appearances, the sun travels around the earth in a daily cycle and also a yearly cycle, so it says in the Word that the sun rises and sets, causing morning, noon, evening, and night and the seasons of spring, summer, fall, and winter—days and years, therefore. The sun, though, is actually immobile. It is an ocean of fire and the earth rotates every day and orbits the sun yearly. People who simply and ignorantly think that the sun is circling the earth do not destroy the physical truth that the earth is rotating on its axis once a day and is borne along its elliptical path every year. However, if they convince themselves that the apparent motion and course of the sun is its true

motion, bringing in support from the Word and the ability to rational-
ize that is inherent in the earthly self, they undermine the actual truth
and even destroy it.

[3] The apparent motion of the sun is a semblance of truth; the
immobility of the sun is a genuine truth. We may talk in terms of the
semblance, and we do so, but thinking that way with conviction weakens
and blinds our ability to think things through rationally.

It is the same with the stars of the nighttime sky. The semblance of
truth is that they too circle us once a day, like the sun; so we say of the
stars too that they rise and set. The real truth, though, is that they are
fixed and that their heaven is immobile. Still, it is allowable for us all to
talk in terms of the way things seem to be.

The reason we are condemned if we convince ourselves of the Word's **96a**
semblances of truth and thereby destroy the inner genuine truth is that
everything in the Word's literal meaning is in communication with heaven
and opens it (see the material in §§62–69 above). This means that when
we use that meaning to justify worldly loves that conflict with heavenly
loves, the inner content of the Word becomes false. As a result, when an
outer (that is, literal) meaning whose inner content is false is communicated to heaven, then heaven is closed because the angels, who treasure the
inner content of the Word, reject it. We can see from this that a false inner
reading, or distorted truth, deprives us of communication with heaven
and closes it. This is why we are condemned if we convince ourselves of
some heretical falsity.

The Word is like a garden that we should refer to as a heavenly para- **96b**
dise in which there are all kinds of delicacies and delights—delicacies in
the form of fruits and delights in the form of flowers—with trees of life
in the middle next to springs of living water. Surrounding this garden,
though, are the trees of a forest. When our religious perspective is based
on divine truths we are in the middle, where the trees of life are, and we
actively enjoy their delicacies and delights. When our religious perspective is based not on truths but only on the [Word's] literal meaning, then
we are on the circumference and all we see is forest. If we are devoted to
the teachings of a false religion and convince ourselves that its teachings
are true, we are not even in the forest; we are outside it, on sand flats
where there is not even any grass.

At some other time I will show that people actually do experience
conditions like this after death.

Further still, we need to realize that the literal meaning of the Word **97**
serves to protect the real truths that lie hidden within it. Its protection

consists of its being susceptible to being turned in different directions and interpreted to agree with our own grasp of it, so that the inner content is not damaged or transgressed. It does no harm if different people understand the literal meaning of the Word differently. It does do harm, though, if the divine truths that lie hidden within are distorted. This in fact does violence to the Word.

To prevent this from happening, the literal meaning offers protection, and it offers protection for people who take for granted the false beliefs of their religion but do not convince themselves that those false beliefs are true. These people do no harm.

[2] This protection is the meaning of angel guardians in the Word, and its description of angel guardians is a depiction of this protection.

This protection is the meaning of the angel guardians stationed at the entrance after Adam and his wife were expelled from the Garden of Eden, of whom we read,

> When Jehovah God drove them out, he made angel guardians dwell to the east of the Garden of Eden, and the flame of a sword turning this way and that, to guard the way of the tree of life. (Genesis 3:24)

The angel guardians mean protection; the way of the tree of life means entrance to the Lord, which we have through the Word; the flame of a sword turning this way and that means divine truth at its very boundaries, which is like the Word in its literal meaning—it too can be turned this way and that.

[3] There is a similar meaning to *the angel guardians of gold placed on top of the two ends of the mercy seat that was on the ark in the tabernacle* (Exodus 25:18–21). Because this was what the angel guardians meant, the Lord talked with Moses between them (Exodus 25:22; 37:9; Numbers 7:89). As noted in §§37–49 above, the Lord does not say anything to us unless it is complete, and divine truth is in its fullness in the literal meaning of the Word; so that is why the Lord talked with Moses between the angel guardians.

The meaning of the *angel guardians on the curtains of the tabernacle and on its veils* (Exodus 26:31) is no different, since the curtains and veils represent the boundaries of heaven and the church and therefore of the Word as well (see §46 above). The meaning of the *angel guardians in the middle of the Jerusalem temple* (1 Kings 6:23–28) and the *angel guardians carved on the walls and gates of the Temple* (1 Kings 6:29, 32, 35) is no different either. The same holds for the *angel guardians in the new temple* (Ezekiel 41:18, 19, 20; again, see §47 above).

[4] Since the angel guardians mean protection that keeps us from going straight to the Lord, heaven, and the divine truth of the Word as it is inwardly, and makes us instead move indirectly through its outermost forms, we read of the King of Tyre,

> You had sealed your full measure and were full of wisdom and perfect in beauty. You were in the Garden of Eden. Every precious stone was your covering. You, angel guardian, were the spreading of a covering. I destroyed you, covering angel guardian, in the midst of stones of fire. (Ezekiel 28:12, 13, 14, 16)

Tyre means the church in respect to its concepts of what is true and good, so the king of Tyre means the Word where these concepts can be found and where they come from. We can see that Tyre and the protecting angel guardians here mean the Word in its outermost form, which is its literal meaning, because it says "you had sealed your full measure," "every precious stone was your covering," and "you, angel guardian, were the spreading of a covering," as well as mentioning a "covering angel guardian." The precious stones that are also mentioned mean truths of the literal meaning of the Word (see §45 above).

Since angel guardians mean the outermost form of divine truth as protection, it says in David,

> Jehovah bowed the heavens and came down, riding upon angel guardians. (Psalms 18:9, 10)

> O Shepherd of Israel, who sits upon the angel guardians, shine forth! (Psalms 80:1)

and

> . . . Jehovah who sits upon the angel guardians. (Psalms 99:1)

To ride and to sit upon angel guardians is [to rest] on the outermost meaning of the Word.

[5] The divine truth in the Word and its nature are described [through correspondences] as angel guardians in chapters 1, 9, and 10 of Ezekiel; but since no one can know what the details of the description mean except those for whom the spiritual meaning has been opened, the meaning of all the things it says about the angel guardians in the first chapter of Ezekiel has been disclosed to me in summary form, as follows:

There is a depiction of the outward divine aura of the Word (verse 4); that aura is represented as a human being (verse 5); it is shown to be united to spiritual and heavenly realities (verse 6). There is a depiction of the nature of the earthly level of the Word (verse 7), and of the nature of the spiritual and heavenly levels of the Word that are united to its earthly level (verses 8, 9). There is a depiction of the divine love within the heavenly, spiritual, and earthly levels of goodness and truth in the Word, together as one and also distinct from one another (verses 10, 11), and an indication that they share a common goal (verse 12). There is a depiction of the aura of the Word that comes from the Lord's divine goodness and divine truth, which give life to the Word (verses 13, 14), of the teachings of what is good and true that are in the Word and from the Word (verses 15–21), and of the divine nature of the Lord that is above it and within it (verses 22, 23) and that comes from it (verses 24, 25). It is shown that the Lord is above the heavens (verse 26) and that to him belong divine love and divine wisdom (verses 27, 28).

These summary statements have been checked against the Word in heaven and are in accord with it.

The Lord Came into the World to Fulfill Everything in the Word and So to Become Divine Truth or the Word Even on the Outermost Level

98 ON the Lord's having come into the world to fulfill everything in the Word, see *Teachings on the Lord* 8–11. As for his having become divine truth or the Word even on the outermost level by this means, that is the meaning of the following statement in John:

> And the Word became flesh and lived among us; and we saw his glory, glory like that of the only-begotten child of the Father. He was full of grace and truth. (John 1:14)

To become flesh is to become the Word even on the outermost level. The disciples were shown his nature as the Word on the outermost level when he was transfigured (Matthew 17:2 and following; Mark 9:2 and following; Luke 9:28 and following). It says there that Moses and Elijah were seen in glory; Moses and Elijah mean the Word (see §48 above).

The Lord as the Word on the outermost level is also described in the first chapter of the Revelation of John, verses 13–16, where all the elements of his description mean the outermost forms of divine truth or the Word.

The Lord had of course been the Word before, but on the very first level, for it says,

> In the beginning was the Word, and the Word was with God, and the Word was God. It was in the beginning with God. (John 1:1, 2)

When the Word became flesh, though, then the Lord became the Word on the outermost level as well. That is why he is called the First and the Last (Revelation 1:8, 11, 17; 2:8; 21:6; 22:13).

The state of the church was completely changed by the Lord's becoming the Word even on the outermost level. All the churches before his Coming were symbolic churches, churches that could see divine truth only in the dark. However, after the Lord's coming into the world, a church was started by him that saw divine truth in the light. The difference is like the difference between evening and morning. In fact, the state of the church before his Coming is called evening, and the state of the church after his Coming is called morning. **99**

Before his coming into the world, the Lord was of course present with the people of the church, but indirectly, through heaven; whereas since his coming into the world he is directly present with the people of the church. This is because he put on a divine earthly form in the world, the form in which he is present with us. The Lord's "glorification" is the complete glorification of the human nature that he took on in the world, and the glorified human form of the Lord is the divine-earthly form.

There are not many people who understand how the Lord is the Word. Yes, they do think that the Lord can enlighten and teach us through the Word, but they do not think that this warrants calling him "the Word." Let them know, though, that each one of us is her or his own distinctive love and therefore that each of us is whatever we have that is good and that is true. That is all that makes us human, and nothing else in us is human. **100**

Every human being is her or his own goodness and truth. That is the reason why angels and spirits, too, are human—because everything good and true that emanates from the Lord is in its proper form human.

The Lord, though, is divine goodness and divine truth itself, so he is the Human, the source of all our humanity.

See *Heaven and Hell* 460 on the human form of everything divinely good and divinely true. This will also be more clearly presented in forthcoming works that are to be about angelic wisdom.

Before the Word That We Have in the World Today, There Was a Word That Has Been Lost

101　BEFORE the Word was given to the Israelite nation through Moses and the prophets, people were familiar with sacrificial worship, and there was prophecy at Jehovah's command. We can tell this from what it says in the books of Moses.

As for their *familiarity with sacrificial worship,* we read that the children of Israel were commanded to overthrow the altars of the nations, shatter their statues, and cut down their groves (Exodus 34:13; Deuteronomy 7:5; 12:3). We also read that at Acacia Grove Israel began to commit whoredom with the daughters of Moab; they summoned people to sacrifices to their gods and the people feasted and bowed down to their gods and especially became attached to the Baal of Peor; and Jehovah became angry with Israel because of this (Numbers 25:1, 2, 3). And Balaam, who was from Syria, had altars built and sacrificed cattle and sheep (Numbers 22:40; 23:1, 2, 14, 29, 30).

[2] As for *there also being prophecy at Jehovah's command,* this we can tell from the prophecies of Balaam (Numbers 23:7–10, 18–24; 24:3–9, 16–24). In fact, he prophesied about the Lord, saying that a star would rise out of Jacob and a scepter out of Israel (Numbers 24:17). As for his prophesying at Jehovah's command, see Numbers 22:13, 18; 23:3, 5, 8, 16, 26; 24:1, 13.

This shows that the nations had divine worship that resembled the worship instituted by Moses for the Israelite nation.

[3] We get a glimpse of the fact that *this was the case even before the time of Abram* from what it says in Moses (Deuteronomy 32:7, 8). It is

clearer, though, in the case of Melchizedek, King of Salem, who brought out bread and wine and blessed Abram, and Abram gave him a tenth of everything he owned (Genesis 14:18–20). Melchizedek represented the Lord, for he is referred to as "a priest to God the Highest" (Genesis 14:18) and it says of the Lord in David, "You are a priest forever after the manner of Melchizedek" (Psalms 110:4). That was why Melchizedek brought out the bread and the wine as holy elements of the church, just as they are in the sacrament of the Holy Supper. It is also why Melchizedek blessed Abram and why Abram gave him a tenth of everything he owned.

Angels of heaven have informed me that the ancients had a Word written entirely in correspondences, but that it was later lost; and they have said that this Word is still preserved among them in heaven and is in use among ancients in the particular heaven where the people live who had that Word when they were living in this world.   **102**

Some of the ancients among whom that Word is still in use in heaven came from the land of Canaan and its adjoining regions—from Syria, for example; from Mesopotamia, Arabia, Chaldea, Assyria; from Egypt; from Sidon, Tyre, and Nineveh—all regions inhabited by people who were devoted to symbolic worship and therefore to the knowledge of correspondences. Their wisdom in those days was based on that knowledge, and by means of it they had an inner perception and communication with the heavens. The ones who were more deeply knowledgeable about the correspondences of that Word were called "the wise" and "the intelligent," though later they were called "diviners" and "magi."

[2] However, since that Word was full of a kind of correspondence that pointed in a remote way to heavenly and spiritual realities and therefore began to be distorted by too many people, in the course of time, under the Lord's divine providence, it vanished and eventually was lost; and they were given another Word composed by means of less remote correspondences. This was done through the prophets among the children of Israel.

All the same, that Word kept many of the place-names in Canaan and in surrounding parts of the Middle East with meanings similar to the ones they had in the earlier Word. That is the reason Abram was ordered to go to that land and why his descendants from Jacob on were brought back into it.

We can tell from the books of Moses that there was a Word among the ancients because he mentioned it and excerpted from it (Numbers 21:14, 15, 27–30). We can tell that the narrative portions of that Word were called *The Wars of Jehovah,* and that the prophetic portions were   **103** called *Pronouncements.* Moses quoted the following from the historical narratives of that Word:

> Therefore it says in *The Book of the Wars of Jehovah,* "Waheb in Suphah and the rivers Arnon, a watercourse of rivers that goes down to [where] Ar is inhabited and rests along the border of Moab." (Numbers 21:14, 15)

In that Word as in ours, the wars of Jehovah were understood to be, and served to describe in detail, the Lord's battles against hell and his victories over it when he would come into the world. These same battles are meant and described time after time in the historical narratives of our Word—in Joshua's battles against the nations of the land of Canaan, for example, and in the wars of the judges and the kings of Israel.

[2] Moses quoted the following from the prophetic portions of that Word:

> Therefore *those who make pronouncements* say, "Come to Heshbon! The city of Sihon will be built up and fortified, because fire has gone out from Heshbon, flame from the city of Sihon. It has devoured Ar of Moab, those who occupy the heights of Arnon. Woe to you, Moab! You have perished, people of Chemosh; he has made his sons fugitives and sent his daughters into captivity to Sihon, king of the Amorites. With arrows we have dealt with them; Heshbon has perished as far as Dibon, and we have spread destruction as far as Nophah, which extends to Medeba." (Numbers 21:27, 28, 29, 30)

Translators change [the title of] this to *Composers of Proverbs,* but it should be called *Makers of Pronouncements* or *Prophetic Pronouncements,* as we can tell from the meaning of the word *moschalim* in Hebrew. It means not only proverbs but also prophetic utterances, as in Numbers 23:7, 18 and 24:3, 15 where it says that Balaam gave forth *his pronouncement,* which was actually a prophetic utterance and was about the Lord. In these instances each of his pronouncements is called a *mashal* in the singular. There is also the fact that what Moses quoted from this source are not proverbs but prophecies.

[3] We can see that this Word was similarly divine or divinely inspired from a passage in Jeremiah where we find almost the same words:

> A fire has gone out from Heshbon and a flame from the midst of Sihon, which has devoured the corner of Moab and the top of the children of tumult. Woe to you, Moab! The people of Chemosh have perished, for

your sons have been carried off into captivity and your daughters into captivity. (Jeremiah 48:45, 46)

Further, both David and Joshua mention another prophetic book of the former Word, *The Book of Jasher* or *The Book of the Righteous One.* Here is where David mentions it:

David lamented over Saul and over Jonathan and wrote, "'To Teach the Children of Judah the Bow.' (You will find this written in *The Book of Jasher.*)" (2 Samuel 1:17, 18)

Here is where Joshua mentions it:

Joshua said, "'Come to rest, O sun, in Gibeon; and, O moon, in the valley of Aijalon.' Is this not written in *The Book of Jasher?*" (Joshua 10:12, 13)

Then too, I have been told that the first seven chapters of Genesis are right there in that ancient Word, so that not the slightest word is missing.

By Means of the Word, There Is Light Even for People Who Are outside the Church and Do Not Have the Word

THERE can be no union with heaven unless somewhere on our **104** planet there is a church where the Word is present and the Lord is known by means of it. This is because the Lord is the God of heaven and earth, and there is no salvation apart from the Lord.

It is adequate if there is simply a church where the Word is present even though that church may consist of relatively few people. Even so, by means of it the Lord is present everywhere in the whole world, because by means of it heaven is united with the human race. As for the union being by means of the Word, see §§62–69 above.

105   I need to explain, though, how the presence and union of the Lord and heaven happens in all lands by means of the Word.

In the Lord's sight, the whole heaven is like one human being, and so is the church (see *Heaven and Hell* 59–86 on the fact that they actually look like a human being to him). In that human being, the church (that is, the church where the Word is read and the Lord is therefore known) functions as the *heart* and as the *lungs*—the [church's] heavenly kingdom as the heart and the [church's] spiritual kingdom as the lungs.

[2] Just as all the other members and organs are maintained and live from these two founts of life in the human body, so too all the people in the various countries of the world who have any religion, worship one God, and live good lives are maintained and live from the union of the Lord and heaven with the church through the Word. By virtue of their faith and life, they are in that human being and reflect its members and organs that are outside the chest cavity where the heart and lungs are. This is because even though the Word in the church may be among relatively few, it gives life from the Lord through heaven to the rest [of the world], just as the heart and lungs give life to the members and organs of the whole body. In fact the sharing is similar.

[3] This is why Christians who read the Word form the chest of that human being. They are at the center, with the Catholics around them; the Muslims who recognize the Lord as the greatest prophet and as the Son of God are around them. Next come the Africans. And the outermost circle is made up of nations and peoples in Asia and in India. There is some further information about this arrangement in §48 of *Last Judgment.*

All the people in that human being face toward the central area where the Christians are.

106   The light is greatest in the central area where the Christians who have the Word are. The explanation is that in the heavens, light is the divine truth that radiates from the Lord as heaven's sun; and since the Word is that truth, we find the most light where we find the people who have the Word.

From there, the light spreads outward from its center, so to speak, to all the surrounding areas, all the way to the boundary, so there is also enlightenment from the Word for nations and peoples outside the church.

On the light in the heavens being the divine truth that radiates from the Lord, and on that light being what gives enlightenment not only to angels but also to us, see *Heaven and Hell* 126–140.

We can conclude that this is characteristic of the whole heaven on the
basis of a similar phenomenon in each community there. This is because
every community of heaven is a heaven in smaller form and is also like a
human being (on this, see *Heaven and Hell* 41–86).

In every community of heaven, the people in the middle similarly
serve as heart and lungs and are the ones who have the most light. From
that middle, that same light and consequent perception of what is true
spread in all directions to the boundaries and therefore to everyone in the
community. This is what makes their spiritual life.

I have been shown that when the people in the middle went away—
the ones who made up the province of the heart and lungs and who had
the most light—the people around them were in darkness and had a perception of what was true that was so slight as to be nearly nonexistent. As
soon as the others came back, though, the light reappeared and they had
their former perception of what was true.

Another experience may serve to illustrate the same thing. There
were some African spirits with me, from Abyssinia. At one point their
ears were opened so that they heard one of the Psalms of David being
sung in a house of worship on earth. This moved them with such pleasure that they joined in the singing. Before long, though, their ears were
closed so that they could not hear anything from that house of worship;
but when that happened they were moved by a pleasure that was even
greater because it was spiritual, and were flooded with understanding at
the same time because the psalm was about the Lord and redemption.
The reason they felt more pleasure was that they were granted communication with the community in heaven that was united with the people
who were singing the psalm in this world. It has become clear to me
from this and from many other experiences that there is communication
with the whole heaven through the Word.

For this reason, there is, by the Lord's divine providence, a universal
interaction between the countries of Europe (especially those where the
Word is read) and the nations outside the church.

We can draw a comparison with the warmth and light of earth's sun,
which nurtures the growth of trees and shrubs even if they stand in the
shadows or under a cloud, as long as the sun rises and appears in the world.
Likewise, heaven's light and warmth is from the Lord as its sun. That light
is the divine truth that is the source of all our intelligence and wisdom,
whether we are angels or people [still in this world]. That is why it says of
the *Word* that it "was with God and was God" and that it "enlightens

everyone who comes into the world" (John 1:1, 9), and that "that light" even "shines in the darkness" (John 1:5).

110 We can tell from this that the Word that is found in the Protestant church enlightens all nations and peoples by means of a spiritual communication, and that the Lord provides that there should always be a church on earth where the Word is read and the Lord is known through it.

So when the Word was virtually cast out by Catholics, divine providence brought about the Reformation, and this meant that the Word was accepted again. Providence also ensured that the Word is regarded as holy by one noble Catholic nation.

111 Because without the Word there is no recognition of the Lord and therefore no salvation, when the Word was utterly distorted and corrupted by the Jewish nation and therefore made virtually null and void, it pleased the Lord to come down from heaven, come into the world, fulfill the Word, and thereby make it whole again, restore it, and give light again to us who live on earth. That is the intent of the Lord's words:

> The people who were sitting in darkness have seen a great light; the light has risen for those who were sitting in the region and shadow of death. (Matthew 4:16; Isaiah 9:2)

112 It was foretold that at the end of the present church darkness would rear up out of the lack of recognition and acknowledgment of the fact that the Lord is the God of heaven and earth and out of the separation of faith from caring. Therefore, to prevent this from leading to the death of any real understanding of the Word, it has now pleased the Lord to unveil the spiritual meaning of the Word and to make it clear that in that meaning—and thereby in the earthly meaning—the Word is all about the Lord and the church. In fact, it is about those subjects alone. He has also unveiled many other things that may serve to restore a light of truth from the Word—a light that has almost been snuffed out.

[2] There are many passages in the Book of Revelation where it predicts that the light of truth would be almost snuffed out at the end of this church. This is also the meaning of these words of the Lord in Matthew:

> Immediately after the affliction of those days the sun will be darkened, the moon will not give its light, the stars will fall from heaven, and the powers of the heavens will be shaken. Then they will see the Son of Humanity coming in the clouds of heaven with glory and power. (Matthew 24:29, 30)

The sun here means love for the Lord; the moon means faith in the Lord; the stars mean concepts from the Lord regarding what is good and true; the Son of Humanity means the Lord as the Word; the clouds mean the Word's literal meaning, and the glory means its spiritual meaning and the way it shines through in the literal meaning.

I have been granted an abundance of experience that has taught me **113** that there is a communication with heaven for us through the Word. When I was reading through the Word from the first chapter of Isaiah to the last of Malachi and the Psalms of David, I was given a clear sense that every verse communicated with a specific community of heaven, and that in this way the whole Word communicated with the entire heaven.

If There Were No Word, No One Would Know about God, Heaven and Hell, Life after Death, and Least of All, about the Lord

THIS follows as a general conclusion from everything that has been **114** said and explained up to this point—that the Word is divine truth itself (§§1–4); the Word is a means of union with heaven's angels (§§62–69); everywhere in the Word there is a marriage of the Lord and the church and therefore a marriage of goodness and truth (§§80–89); the quality of a church depends on the quality of its understanding of the Word (§§76–79); the Word exists in the heavens as well, and it is the source of angels' wisdom (§§70–75); there is spiritual light through the Word for nations and peoples outside the church as well (§§104–113); and more. From this we may conclude that if it were not for the Word, no one would have a spiritual understanding. That is, no one would know about God, heaven and hell, and life after death; and there would be absolutely no knowledge about the Lord and about faith in him and love for him. This means there would be no knowledge of redemption, though this is the means to salvation.

The Lord said to his disciples, "Without me you cannot do anything" (John 15:5), and John [the Baptist] said, "People cannot receive anything unless it has been given to them from heaven" (John 3:27).

115 But then there are people who propose and then prove to themselves that without the Word we could know about the existence of God, about heaven and hell, too, and something about other things that the Word teaches. They then use this assumption to undermine the authority and holiness of the Word, if not out loud, then in their hearts. There is no dealing with them on the basis of the Word. We must appeal to the light of reason because they do not believe the Word, only themselves.

If you look into it with the light of reason you will discover that human beings possess two faculties of life, called will and understanding, and that our understanding is subject to our will, while our will is not subject to our understanding. All our understanding does is teach and show us the way.

Look further, and you will discover that our will involves a sense of our own self-importance; that in and of itself, this self-importance is nothing but evil; and that it gives rise to falsity in our understanding.

[2] Once you have discovered this, you will see that on our own we do not *want* to understand anything except what follows from our will, and that we would not *be able* to understand anything else if there were no external basis of our knowing. On the basis of the self-importance associated with our will, we do not want to understand anything that does not focus on ourselves and the world. Anything higher is in darkness for us. When we see the sun, the moon, and the stars, for example, and we happen to think about their origin, can we come up with any thought but that they brought themselves into being? Can we raise our thoughts higher than those of many of this world's scholars, who believe that nature created itself even though they know from the Word that God created everything? What would they think, then, if they knew nothing from the Word?

[3] Do you think that the ancient sages, including Aristotle, Cicero, Seneca, and others who wrote about God and the immortality of the soul, picked this up first from themselves? No, it was from others, who had it handed down to them from still others who first learned it from the Word.

Writers of natural theology, too, do not get anything like this from themselves. They are only using rational means to support what they have learned from the church, where the Word is found—and there may be some among them who vocally support it but nevertheless do not believe.

I have been allowed to see people born on [remote] islands who were **116** rational in civic matters but knew absolutely nothing about God. In the spiritual world they look like apes and lead an almost apelike life; but since they were born human and have the ability to accept spiritual life, they are taught by angels and brought to life by recognizing that the Lord is human.

What we are like left to our own devices is obvious from people in hell. This includes some of the eminent and learned who are unwilling to hear anything about God and therefore cannot pronounce the word "God." I have seen them and talked with them, and have also talked with some who burst into flaming wrath and rage when they hear anyone talking about God.

[2] Stop and think, then, what people would be like who had never heard about God, when there are people like this who have heard about God, who have written about God, and who have preached about God. Many people of this sort are Jesuits.

The basic cause of this kind of nature is a will that is evil; and this, as already noted [§115], leads our understanding and takes away any truth it has from the Word. If it is possible for us to know on our own that God exists and that we go on living after death, why then do some people not know that we remain human beings after death? Why do some believe that the soul or spirit is like the wind or the ether, and does not see with its own eyes or hear with its own ears or speak with its own mouth before it is [once again] united and merged with its body, even though that is now a cadaver or even a skeleton?

[3] So imagine a theory of worship concocted solely in the light of reason. Would it not teach that we ourselves are to be worshiped, as has been done for ages and still is by people, despite the fact that they know from the Word that we should worship God alone? No other kind of worship can come from our own self-aggrandizement, not even the worship of the sun and the moon.

As for the fact that there has been religion from the earliest times **117** and that people all over the world have known about God and have known something about life after death, this did not come from the people themselves and from their own mental acuity, but from that former Word discussed in §§101–103 above, and later from the Israelite Word. Religious principles spread from these sources into southeast Asia, including its islands; through Egypt and Ethiopia into Africa; and from the coast of Asia Minor into Greece and from there into Italy.

But since there was no way the Word could be composed except in the language of representative imagery, in images of things characteristic of this world that corresponded to and therefore signified heavenly realities, the religions of many nations were turned into idolatries—in Greece into fables—and divine attributes and characteristics were turned into individual gods led by one highest God whom people called Jove, from "Jehovah." It is common knowledge that [ancient people] were familiar with paradise, the Flood, sacred fire, and the four ages—from the first Golden Age to the last Iron Age—which serve in the Word to mean the four states of the church, as in Daniel 2:31–35.

It is also common knowledge that Islam, which came later and wiped out the preceding religious cultures of many nations, was drawn from the Word of both Testaments.

118 Let me say in closing what people are like after death if they have attributed everything to their own intelligence and little if anything to the Word. At first they seem to be drunk, then foolish, and finally brainless; and they sit in darkness. So beware of this kind of insanity in yourselves.

The White Horse

Described in

Revelation 19

Followed by Material on

the Word and Its Spiritual or Inner Meaning

Drawn from Secrets of Heaven

The White Horse
Described in Revelation 19

I N the Book of Revelation, this is how John describes the Word in regard to its spiritual or inner meaning:

> I saw heaven opened, and behold, a white horse. And the one who sat on it was called faithful and true, and with justice he judges and makes war. His eyes were a flame of fire, and on his head were many gems. He had a name written that no one knew except him. He was clothed with a robe dipped in blood, and his name is called *the Word of God*. The armies in heaven, clothed in fine linen, white and clean, followed him on white horses. He has on his robe and on his thigh a name written: *King of Kings and Lord of Lords.* (Revelation 19:11, 12, 13, 14, 16)

Only from the inner meaning can anyone know what these particular details involve. It is obvious that each one represents and means something—the heaven that is opened; the horse that is white; the one who sat on it; his judging and making war justly; his eyes being a flame of fire; his having many gems on his head; his having a name that no one knew except him; his being clothed with a robe dipped in blood; the armies in heaven, clothed in fine linen, white and clean, following him on white horses; and his having a name written on his robe and on his thigh. It says plainly that this is the Word and that it is the Lord who is the Word, since it says "his name is called *the Word of God"* and then says "he has on his robe and on his thigh a name written: *King of Kings and Lord of Lords."*

[2] If we interpret the individual words, we can see that this is describing the spiritual or inner meaning of the Word. *Heaven being opened* represents and means that the inner meaning of the Word is seen in heaven and therefore is seen by people in this world to whom heaven has been opened. The *horse that is white* represents and means an understanding of the Word in regard to its deeper contents (the reason for this meaning of the white horse will become clear in what follows). Unquestionably, the *one who sat on the horse* is the Lord as the Word and is therefore the Word, since it says "his name is called the Word of God." He is described as *faithful* and *judging justly* because he is good, and he is described as *true* and *making war justly* because he is true, since the Lord himself is justice. His *eyes being a flame of fire* means the divine truth that comes from the divine goodness of his divine love. His *having many gems on his head* means all the types of goodness and truth that belong to faith. His *having a name written that no one knew except him* means that what the Word is like in its inner meaning is seen by no one except him and those to whom he reveals it. His *being clothed with a robe dipped in blood* means the Word in its literal meaning, which has suffered violence. The *armies in heaven that followed him on white horses* mean the people who have an understanding of the deeper contents of the Word. Their *being clothed in fine linen, white and clean,* means that these people have an awareness of truth that comes from doing good. His *having a name written on his robe and on his thigh* means what is true and what is good, and what that truth and goodness are like.

[3] We can see from this and from what precedes and follows [this passage in the Word] that we have here a prediction that around the last time of the church the spiritual or inner meaning of the Word will be opened. What will happen then is described in verses 17, 18, 19, 20, 21.

There is no need to demonstrate here that this is the meaning of these words, since the details have been explained in *Secrets of Heaven* as follows:

The Lord is the Word because he is divine truth: 2533, 2813, 2894, 5272, 8535. The Word is divine truth: 4692, 5075, 9987. It says that the one who sat on the horse judges and makes war justly because the Lord is justice; the Lord is called "justice" because he saved the human race by his own power: 1813, 2025, 2026, 2027, 9715, 9809, 10019, 10152. Justice is a form of merit that belongs to the Lord alone: 9715, 9979. His eyes being a flame of fire means divine truth that comes from the divine goodness of his divine love, because eyes mean understanding and mean the truth that belongs to faith: 2701, 4403–4421, 4523–4534, 6923, 9051, 10569; and a flame of fire means the goodness of love: 934, 4906, 5215, 6314, 6832. The gems on his head mean all the types of goodness and truth that belong to faith: 114, 3858, 6335, 6640, 9863, 9865, 9868, 9873, 9905. His having a name written that no one knew except him means that no one sees what the Word is like in its inner meaning except him and those to whom he reveals it, because the name means what the named thing is really like: 144, 145, 1754, 1896, 2009, 2724, 3006, 3237, 3421, 6674, 9310. His being clothed with a robe dipped in blood means the Word in its literal meaning, which has suffered violence, because a garment means truth since truth clothes what is good: 1073, 2576, 5248, 5319, 5954, 9212, 9216, 9952, 10536 (and this has particular reference to the most external forms of truth and therefore to the Word in its letter: 5248, 6918, 9158, 9212); and because blood means the violence inflicted on what is true by what is false: 374, 1005, 4735, 5476, 9127. The armies in heaven that followed him on white horses mean the people who have an understanding of the deeper contents of the Word, because armies mean people who have the understanding of truth and the love for doing good that are characteristic of heaven and the church: 3448, 7236, 7988, 8019; a horse means understanding: 3217, 5321, 6125, 6400, 6534, 6534, 7024, 8146, 8381; and white means truth that is in heaven's light and therefore means deeper truth: 3301, 3993, 4007, 5319. Their being clothed in fine linen, white and clean, means that these people have an awareness of truth that comes from doing good, because linen or fine linen means truth of a heavenly origin, which is truth arising from what is good: 5319, 9469. His having a name written on his robe and on his thigh means what is true and what is good, and what that truth and goodness are like, because a robe means what is true and a name means what that truth is like (as noted above), and the thigh means goodness that comes from love: 3021, 4277, 4280, 9961, 10488. King of Kings and Lord of Lords is the Lord in respect to divine truth and in respect to divine goodness. The Lord is called "King" because of his divine truth: 3009, 5068, 6148. He is called "Lord" because of his divine goodness: 4973, 9167, 9194.

We can see from this what the Word is like in its spiritual or inner meaning and that there is not a word in it that does not mean something spiritual, something about heaven and the church.

Horses are often mentioned in the prophetic books of the Word, but **2** until now no one has been aware that a horse means understanding and its rider means someone who is intelligent. This is perhaps because it seems strange and bewildering to say that a horse has this kind of meaning when spiritually understood, and therefore has this kind of meaning in the Word. There is support for this, however, in many passages in the Word, of which I should like here to cite only a few. In Israel's prophecy about Dan:

> Dan will be a serpent on the way, a darting serpent on the path, that bites the horse's heels, and its rider falls backward. (Genesis 49:17, 18)

No one will understand the meaning of this prophecy about one of the tribes of Israel who does not know the meaning of a serpent and of a horse and a rider. No one can fail to know, though, that something spiritual is involved. You may see what these particular things mean in *Secrets of Heaven* 6398, 6399, 6400, 6401, where this prophecy is explained. In Habakkuk:

> God, you are riding on your horses; your chariots are salvation. You walked through the sea with your horses. (Habakkuk 3:8, 15)

We can see that horses here mean something spiritual because these things are being said of God. Otherwise, what would be involved in God riding on his horses and walking through the sea with his horses?

The same holds true for Zechariah 14:20: "On that day 'Holiness belongs to Jehovah' will be engraved on the bells of the horses"; and for Zechariah 12:4, 5: "'On that day,' says Jehovah, 'I will strike every horse with confusion and its rider with madness. I will open my eyes on the house of Judah and strike every horse of the people with blindness.'" This is about the purging of the church that happens when there is no longer any understanding of what is true, so it is described in terms of horse and rider. Otherwise, what would be involved in striking every horse with confusion and striking every horse of the people with blindness? What does this have to do with the church? In Job:

> [Because] God deprived [the ostrich] of wisdom and did not endow her with understanding, when she lifts herself up on high, she scorns the horse and its rider. (Job 39:17, 18, 19, and following)

Here it is obvious that the horse means understanding. This is also the case in David when it speaks of "riding on the word of truth" (Psalms 45:4) and in many other passages.

Further, who would know why Elijah and Elisha were called "the chariot of Israel and its cavalry" and why Elisha's servant saw the mountain full of horses and chariots of fire if they did not know what a chariot and a cavalry mean and what Elijah and Elisha represent? For Elisha said to Elijah, "My father, my father, the chariot of Israel and its cavalry" (2 Kings 2:11, 12); and King Joash said to Elisha, "My father, my father, the chariot of Israel and its cavalry" (2 Kings 13:14); and it says of Elisha's servant, "Jehovah opened the eyes of Elisha's servant, and he saw. And behold, the mountain was full of horses and chariots of fire all around Elisha" (2 Kings 6:17).

The reason Elijah and Elisha were called the chariot of Israel and its cavalry is that both represent the Lord as the Word, the chariot meaning a body of teaching drawn from the Word and the cavalry meaning understanding. On Elijah and Elisha as representing the Lord as the Word, see *Secrets of Heaven* 5247, 7643, 8029, 9372; and on a chariot as meaning a body of teaching drawn from the Word see §§5321, 8215.

A horse means understanding because of the way things are represented in the spiritual world. People there often see horses, and people sitting on horses, and also chariots, and everyone there knows that they mean matters of understanding and refer to a body of teaching. I have often seen that when people there were using their understanding to think, they appeared as if they were riding horses. That is how their thought process presented itself to others, even though they themselves were unaware of it. **3**

There is also a meeting place there for large numbers of people who ponder theological truths with their understanding and talk about them. When others come there, they see that whole area full of chariots and horses; and newcomers who wonder why this is happening are informed that this sight is caused by the deep thought that is occurring. The place is called "the Assembly of the Intelligent and the Wise."

I have also seen shining horses and fiery chariots when particular people were being taken up into heaven, which was a sign that they were being taken up because they had then been taught about heavenly theological truths and had come to understand them.

Seeing this brought to my mind the meaning of the chariot of fire and the horses of fire by which Elijah was taken up into heaven [2 Kings 2:11–12] and of the horses and chariots of fire that Elisha's servant saw when his eyes were opened [2 Kings 6:17].

It was common knowledge in the ancient churches that this is what chariots and horses meant, because they were representative churches; for the people of those churches, the knowledge of symbolism and representations was the primary form of knowledge. The meaning of a horse as understanding spread from these churches to the wise in surrounding lands, especially into Greece. This led to the practice of characterizing the **4** sun, where they placed their god of wisdom and intelligence, as riding in a chariot drawn by four fiery horses.

Not only that, when they described the god of the sea, since the sea meant the store of knowledge that arises from the understanding, they gave him horses, too; and when they described the way knowledge arises from the understanding, they imagined a winged horse that broke open with its hoof a spring attended by nine virgins, who were the various types of knowledge. In fact, they knew from the ancient churches that a horse meant understanding, that wings meant spiritual truth, that a hoof meant something factual arising from the understanding, and that a spring meant a theological principle that gave rise to knowledge. The Trojan horse stood for a thing contrived specifically by the understanding, the purpose of which was to breach walled defenses.

Even today, when it comes to describing understanding, some people borrow from the accepted custom of the ancients the practice of using the image of a flying horse, Pegasus, and of describing teachings as a wellspring and the various types of knowledge as virgins. Hardly anyone realizes, though, that in a mystical sense a horse *means* understanding, let alone that these meanings have spread from the early, symbolic churches to people who were not part of those churches.

5 Because the white horse means an understanding of the Word in its spiritual or inner meaning, what now follow are statements about the Word and about that meaning presented in *Secrets of Heaven,* since in that work everything in Genesis and Exodus is explained in terms of the spiritual or inner meaning of the Word.

The Word and Its Spiritual or Inner Meaning
from *Secrets of Heaven*

*T*HE *necessity and excellence of the Word.* From earthly light, we **6** know nothing about the Lord, heaven and hell, our life after death, or the divine truths that are essential for our spiritual and eternal life: 8944, 10318, 10319, 10320. Evidence for this is the fact that many people, including scholars, do not believe in these things even though they were born where the Word is present and have been taught from it about these matters: 10319. That is why it became necessary for there to be some revelation from heaven, since we are born for heaven: 1775. For this reason there has been a revelation in every era: 2895. Information about the various kinds of revelation in this world over time: 10355, 10632. The earliest people, the ones who lived before the Flood, whose era was called the Golden Age, had direct revelation and therefore had divine truth written on their hearts: 2896. The ancient churches that existed after the Flood had a Word containing both historical and prophetic material: 2686, 2897. (See *The New Jerusalem and Its Teachings* 247 for information about these churches.) Its historical materials were called *The Wars of Jehovah* and its prophetic materials were called *Pronouncements:* 2897. This Word was like our own Word as far as its inspiration was concerned, but it was accommodated to those churches: 2897. It was mentioned by Moses: 2686, 2897. However, this Word has been lost: 2897. There were also prophetic revelations among other peoples, as we can see from Balaam's prophecies [Numbers 23–24]: 2898.

[2] The Word is divine throughout and in every detail: 639, 3305, 10321, 10637. The Word is divine and holy down to the smallest letters and the tip of every letter: 9349 (which includes evidence from eyewitness experience). How people nowadays explain the claim that the Word is inspired down to the smallest letters: 1886.

[3] The church takes a particular form where the Word exists and the Lord is known by means of it, and therefore where divine truths have been revealed: 3857, 10761. Still, though, this does not mean that people are part of the church by merely being born where the Word exists and the Lord is known by means of it; people are part of the church only if they are being regenerated by the Lord by means of truths from the

Word—that is, they are living lives of love and faith: 6637, 10143, 10153, 10578, 10645, 10829.

7   *The Word is understood only by people who are enlightened.* Our rational capacity cannot grasp things that are divine; it cannot even grasp things that are spiritual unless it is enlightened by the Lord: 2196, 2203, 2209, 2654. This means that only enlightened people can understand the Word: 10323. The Lord makes it possible for people who are enlightened to understand what is true and to sort out things that seem contradictory: 9382, 10659. Understood on a literal level, the Word is not consistent and often seems self-contradictory (9025); therefore people who are not enlightened can interpret it and constrain it to support all kinds of opinions and heresies and to favor all kinds of worldly and bodily loves (4783, 10330, 10400). We gain enlightenment from the Word if we read it out of a love for what is true and good, but not if we read it out of a love for fame, profit, or prestige, and therefore out of a love for ourselves: 9382, 10548, 10549, 10550. We are enlightened if we are committed to living good lives and therefore are affected by what is true: 8694. We are enlightened if our inner self has been opened—that is, if our inner self is capable of being raised into heaven's light: 10400, 10402, 10691, 10694. Enlightenment is an actual opening of the deeper reaches of our minds as well as a raising of them into heaven's light: 10330. If we regard the Word as holy, then without our knowing it something holy flows in from within us—that is, through our inner self from the Lord: 6789. We are enlightened and see truths in the Word if we are being led by the Lord, but not if we are leading ourselves: 10638. We are being led by the Lord when we love what is true because it is true; that is, when we love to live by divine truths: 10578, 10645, 10829. The Word is brought to life for us depending on the amount of life there is in our love and faith: 1776. The products of a self-oriented intelligence have no life in them, because nothing good comes from our self-centeredness: 8941, 8944. We cannot be enlightened if we have thoroughly convinced ourselves of false teachings: 10640.

[2] It is our understanding that is enlightened: 6608, 9300. Our understanding is what receives truth: 6222, 6608, 10659. For every teaching of the church, how well we understand it depends on the nature of the concepts we have of it in our intellect and in our thinking: 3310, 3825. As long as we are living in this world, our concepts are earthly because we are thinking on an earthly level. However, there are spiritual concepts hidden within them if we are passionately interested in the truth for its own sake, and these concepts become ours after death: 3310, 5510, 6201,

10236, 10240, 10551. If we cannot conceive of something in our intellect and in our thinking, we cannot comprehend it, either: 3825. Our concepts of matters of faith are disclosed in the other life, and angels there see what our concepts are like; we are then united with others in keeping with our concepts, provided that they are rooted in love and affection: 1869, 3310, 5510, 6200, 6201, 8885. This means that the Word is understood only by rational people, since without some concept of a subject and some rational insight, "believing" is only keeping in our memory some statement that we do not comprehend or love. This is not believing: 2533. It is the literal meaning of the Word that is enlightened for us: 3436, 9824, 9905, 10548.

The Word is understood only by means of a body of teaching drawn from the Word. The church's body of teaching must be drawn from the Word: 3464, 5402, 5432, 10763, 10765. Without a body of teaching, the Word is not intelligible: 9025, 9409, 9424, 9430, 10324, 10431, 10582. A true body of teaching is a lamp for us when we read the Word: 10400. Any authentic body of teaching must come from people who are enlightened by the Lord: 2510, 2516, 2519, 9424, 10105. The Word is to be understood by means of a body of teaching constructed by someone who is enlightened: 10324. People in a state of enlightenment construct a body of teaching for themselves from the Word: 9382, 10659. The nature of the difference between people who teach and learn on the basis of the church's body of teaching and those who do so solely on the basis of the literal meaning of the Word: 9025. People who are focused on the literal meaning of the Word without having a body of teaching do not arrive at any understanding of divine truths: 9409, 9410, 10582. They fall into many errors: 10431. When people who have a passionate interest in the truth for its own sake reach adulthood and can see things with their own understanding, they do not simply rest in the theological tenets of their church but check them carefully against the Word to see whether they are true: 5402, 5432, 6047. Otherwise, what everyone believes could be declared true merely because someone else said so or because it was the religion of the person's native soil, whether that person was born Jewish or Greek: 6047. Nevertheless, principles that have become matters of faith on the basis of the Word's literal meaning should not be eliminated unless they have been fully examined: 9039.

[2] The church's true body of teaching is made up of teachings focused on caring and faith: 2417, 4766, 10763, 10764. What makes a church is not a body of teaching about faith but living according to faith, which means caring: 809, 1798, 1799, 1834, 4468, 4672, 4766, 5826, 6637. A body

of teaching is nothing unless its teachings are lived; anyone can see that they exist to be lived by, not just to be committed to memory and then given some thought: 1515, 2049, 2116. In today's churches there is a body of teaching focused on faith and not on caring, and the body of teaching focused on caring has been consigned to the discipline known as moral theology: 2417. The church would be united if individuals were recognized as members of the church on the basis of their lives and therefore of their caring: 1285, 1316, 2982, 3267, 3445, 3451, 3452. How much more valid a body of teaching focused on caring is than a body of teaching focused on faith separated from caring: 4844. If we know nothing about caring, then we know nothing about heaven: 4783. If we have a body of teaching focused only on faith and not on caring at the same time, we lapse into errors: 2383, 2417, 3146, 3325, 3412, 3413, 3416, 3773, 4672, 4730, 4783, 4925, 5351, 7623–7627, 7752–7762, 7790, 8094, 8313, 8530, 8765, 9186, 9224, 10555 (which include some discussion of the errors in question). [In the ancient church,] people who were devoted to teachings on faith but not to living according to faith, which means caring, were called "the uncircumcised" or "Philistines": 3412, 3413, 3463, 8313, 8093, 9340. The early people had a body of teaching focused on love for the Lord and caring about their neighbor, and their teachings about faith were subsidiary to it: 2417, 3419, 4844, 4955.

[3] Once a body of teaching has been constructed by someone who is enlightened, it can then be supported by rational and factual means; in this way it is more fully understood, and this strengthens it: 2553, 2719, 3052, 3310, 6047. (There is more on this subject in *The New Jerusalem and Its Teachings* 51.) People who are committed to faith separated from caring want the church's body of teaching simply to be believed without any rational inquiry: 3394.

[4] The practice of wisdom is not to support a dogma blindly but to see whether or not the dogma is true before convincing ourselves of its truth; this is what people do when they enjoy enlightenment: 1017, 4741, 7012, 7680, 7950. The light that is shed by convincing ourselves is an earthly light, not a spiritual one, and it is accessible even to evil people: 8780. We can convince ourselves of anything, even something false, in such a way that it seems to be true: 2477, 5033, 6865, 8521.

9 *There is a spiritual meaning in the Word that is known as "the inner meaning."* No one who does not know what correspondence is can know what the spiritual or inner meaning of the Word is: 2895, 4322. Absolutely everything in the earthly world, right down to the smallest details, corresponds to and therefore means something spiritual: 2987–3003, 3213–3227.

The spiritual realities to which earthly things correspond take on different guises on the earthly level and therefore are not recognized: 1887, 3632, 8920. Hardly anyone knows where in the Word its divine quality resides, when in fact it is in its inner or spiritual meaning—and people nowadays do not even know that this meaning exists: 4989, 9280. The mystical dimension of the Word is precisely that the contents of its inner or spiritual meaning deal with the Lord, the glorification of his human nature, his kingdom, and the church, and not with earthly things that take place in this world: 4923. In many passages the statements of the prophets are unintelligible and therefore of no use apart from their inner meaning: 2608, 8020, 8398 (which provide some examples). For example, the meaning of the white horse in the Book of Revelation (2760 and following); the meaning of the keys of the kingdom of the heavens that were given to Peter (preface to Genesis 22, §9410); the meaning of flesh, blood, bread, and wine in the Holy Supper (8682); the meaning of Jacob's prophecies about his sons in Genesis 49 (6306, 6333–6465); the meanings of many of the prophecies about Judah and Israel, prophecies that in their literal meaning contradict each other and do not square with [the actual history of] that people (6333, 6361, 6415, 6438, 6444); and countless other passages (2608). More on what correspondence is may be found in *Heaven and Hell* 87–102, 103–115, 303–310.

An overview of the inner or spiritual meaning of the Word: 1767–1777, 1869–1879. There is deeper meaning throughout the Word and in every detail of it: 1143, 1984, 2135, 2333, 2395, 2495, 2619. These meanings are not visible in the literal meaning, but they are there within: 4442.

The inner meaning of the Word is primarily for angels, but it is also for us. To explain what the inner meaning of the Word is, what its nature is, and what its source is, I need to offer the following overview.

People think and speak differently in heaven than in this world—those in heaven think and speak in a spiritual way, and those in this world think and speak in an earthly way. As a result, when we are reading the Word, the angels who are with us take spiritually what we are taking in an earthly way. This means that angels are focused on the Word's inner meaning while we are focused on its outer meaning. However, the two make a single meaning because of their correspondence.

Angels not only think spiritually, they also talk spiritually. Further, they are with us and are united to us through the Word. On these matters see *Heaven and Hell* where it deals with the wisdom of heaven's angels (§§265–275), their speech (§§234–245), and their union with us (§§291–302), a union that takes place by means of the Word (§§303–310).

[2] The Word is understood differently by angels in the heavens than by us on earth; the meaning accessible to angels is an inner or spiritual one, while the meaning accessible to us is outer or earthly: 1887, 2395. Angels are aware of the inner meaning of the Word and not its outer meaning: 1769, 1770, 1771, 1772 (which include evidence from personal experience with angels who spoke with me from heaven while I was reading the Word). Angelic concepts and angelic speech are both spiritual, while our concepts and speech are earthly, so the inner meaning, being spiritual, is for angels: 2333 (which includes evidence from eyewitness experience). Even so, the literal meaning of the Word serves as a support for the spiritual concepts of angels, much the way the words of our language carry the meaning of a subject for us: 2143. Matters of the Word's inner meaning fall into the category of things visible in heaven's light and therefore are suited to angelic perception: 2618, 2619, 2629, 3086. As a result, what angels get from the Word is very precious to them: 2540, 2541, 2545, 2551. Angels do not understand even a single word of the literal meaning of the Word: 64, 65, 1434, 1929. They do not know the names of people or places in the Word, either: 1434, 1888, 4442, 4480. Names cannot enter heaven or be pronounced there: 1876, 1888. All the names in the Word denote actual things, and are changed into concepts of those things in heaven: 768, 1888, 4310, 4442, 5225, 5287, 10329. Further, angels think in terms of qualities without reference to individuals: 5287, 8343, 8985, 9007. Examples from the Word showing the elegance of its inner meaning even when it consists of nothing but names: 1224, 1888, 5095. Further, a long list of names sometimes expresses just one topic in its inner meaning: 5095. All numbers in the Word have definable meanings as well: 482, 487, 647, 648, 755, 813, 1963, 1988, 2075, 2252, 3252, 4264, 6175, 9488, 9659, 10217, 10253. To the extent that their inner reaches are opened into heaven, spirits as well perceive the inner meaning of the Word: 1771. The literal meaning of the Word, which is earthly, is transformed instantly into spiritual meaning for angels because there is a correspondence (5648); and this happens apart from any hearing or awareness on their part of the content of the literal or outer meaning (10215). So the literal or outer meaning exists only on our level and does not reach beyond it: 2015.

[3] There is an inner meaning of the Word and also an inmost or highest meaning: 9407, 10604, 10614, 10627 (which include some discussion). Spiritual angels (that is, angels in the Lord's spiritual kingdom) perceive the inner meaning of the Word, and heavenly angels (that is, angels in the Lord's heavenly kingdom) perceive its inmost meaning: 2157, 2275.

[4] The Word is for us and is also for angels; it has been accommodated to each: 7381, 8862, 10322. The Word is what unites heaven and
earth: 2310, 2895, 9212, 9216, 9357. The joining of heaven to us is brought
about by means of the Word: 9396, 9400, 9401, 10452. That is why the
Word is called "a covenant": 9396. In fact, "covenant" means a joining
together: 665, 666, 1023, 1038, 1864, 1996, 2003, 2021, 6804, 8767, 8778,
9396, 10632. There is an inner meaning in the Word because the Word
came down to us from the Lord through the three heavens (2310, 6597);
and in this way it was adapted to the angels of the three heavens and also
to us (7381, 8862). This is why the Word is divine (4989, 9280), and is
holy (10276), and spiritual (4480), and is inspired by the Divine (9094).
This is what inspiration is: 9094.

[5] People who have been regenerated, too, are effectively engaged
with the Word's inner meaning even though they do not realize it, since
their inner self is open, and this self has spiritual perception: 10400. However, the spiritual content of the Word flows into earthly concepts for
them and therefore presents itself in earthly terms, because as long as we
are living in this world, as far as we can tell we do our thinking in the
earthly self: 5614. This means that for people who are enlightened, the
light of truth comes from within, that is, through their inner selves from
the Lord: 10691, 10694. Something holy also flows in by this path for
people who regard the Word as holy: 6789. Since regenerate people are
(without knowing it) effectively engaged with the Word's inner meaning
and with its holiness, after death they come into that meaning sponta-
neously and are no longer engaged with the literal meaning: 3226, 3342,
3343. The concepts of our inner self are spiritual, but while we are living
in this world we are not aware of them because they are within our earthly
thinking, giving it the ability to reason: 10236, 10240, 10551. After death,
though, we come into consciousness of our own inner concepts because
they are proper to our spirit, and they are then the source not only of our
thinking but also of our speech: 2470, 2472, 2476, 10568, 10604. That is
why I said that people who have been regenerated are unaware that they
are engaged with the Word's spiritual meaning, although it is actually the
source of their enlightenment.

There are countless treasures hidden in the inner or spiritual meaning of **11**
the Word. In its inner meaning, the Word contains countless things that
are beyond our grasp: 3085, 3086. They also cannot be put into words or
explained: 1955. They are manifest only to angels and are understood only
by them: 167. The inner meaning of the Word contains hidden treasures
of heaven that have to do with the Lord and his kingdom in the heavens

and on earth: 1, 2, 3, 4, 937. These treasures are not visible in the literal meaning: 937, 1502, 2161. Many of the things in the prophets that seem random come together coherently in a beautiful sequence in the inner meaning: 7153, 9022.

There is not a single word in the literal meaning of the Word—not even the smallest letter—that can be lost in the Word's original language without causing a break in the inner meaning, so this is why, in the Lord's divine providence, the Word has been so completely preserved, right down to the tip of every letter: 7933. There are countless things within the details of the Word (6617, 6620, 8920), and in every word (1869). There are countless things in the Lord's Prayer and in its details (6619), and in the Ten Commandments, though their outer meaning contains things that were known to every people quite apart from any revelation (8862, 8902). There is something holy in the tip of every letter of the Word in its original language. See evidence of this presented in *Heaven and Hell* 260, where there is an explanation of the Lord's words "Not one little letter or the tip of one letter will pass from the law" (Matthew 5:18).

[2] In the Word, especially in the prophetic books, there are what seem to be paired expressions of the same idea, but one refers to what is good and the other to what is true: 683, 707, 2516, 8339. Teachings about goodness and teachings about truth are wondrously joined to each other in the Word, but this joining is visible only to people who know about its inner meaning: 10554. Therefore in the Word as a whole and in its details there is a divine marriage and a heavenly marriage: 683, 793, 801, 2173, 2516, 2712, 5138, 7022. The divine marriage is the marriage of divine goodness and divine truth and is therefore the Lord in heaven, in whom alone this marriage exists there: 3004, 3005, 3009, 4137, 5194, 5502, 6343, 7945, 8339, 9263, 9314. "Jesus" means divine goodness and "Christ" means divine truth, and together they mean the divine marriage in heaven: 3004, 3005, 3009. This marriage is in the details of the Word in its inner meaning, so the Lord is there with his divine goodness and divine truth: 5502. What is called the heavenly marriage is the marriage of goodness and truth that comes from the Lord in heaven and in the church: 2508, 2618, 2803, 3004, 3211, 3952, 6179. So in this respect the Word is a kind of heaven: 2173, 10126. Heaven is compared to a marriage in the Word because of the marriage of goodness and truth there: 2758, 3132, 4434, 4835.

[3] The inner meaning contains the genuine teachings of the church: 9025, 9430, 10400. People who understand the Word in its inner meaning know the true teachings of the church, because the inner meaning

contains them: 9025, 9430, 10400. The inner reality of the Word is also the inner reality of the church, as well as the inner reality of worship: 10460. The Word is a body of teaching focused on love for the Lord and caring about our neighbor: 3419, 3420.

[4] The Word in its literal meaning is like a cloud, while in its inner meaning it is glory (preface to Genesis 18, §§5922, 6343, in explanation of the statement that "the Lord is going to come in the clouds of heaven, with glory" [Matthew 24:30; Mark 13:26; Luke 21:27]). Further, "clouds" in the Word means the Word in its literal meaning, and "glory" means the Word in its inner meaning: preface to Genesis 18, §§4060, 4391, 5922, 6343, 6752, 8106, 8781, 9430, 10551, 10574. Compared to the contents of the inner meaning, the contents of the literal meaning are like the distorted images around a polished optical cylinder that actually present a beautiful image of a person on the cylinder: 1871. People in the spiritual world who want and acknowledge only the literal meaning are represented by misshapen old women, while people who want and acknowledge the inner meaning as well are represented by beautifully dressed young women: 1774. The Word in its fullness is an image of heaven because the Word is divine truth, and divine truth is what makes heaven; and since heaven is like one individual, the Word is in this respect like an image of a person: 1871. *Heaven, grasped as a single entity, reflects a single individual* (*Heaven and Hell* 59–67), *and divine truth emanating from the Lord is what makes heaven* (*Heaven and Hell* 7–12, 126–140, 200–212). The inner meaning of the Word is presented to angels' view in a beautiful and pleasing way: 1767, 1768. The literal meaning is like a body, and the inner meaning is like the soul of that body: 8943. The life of the Word therefore comes from its inner meaning: 1405, 4857. The Word is pure in its inner meaning, although it does not seem to be so in its literal meaning: 2362, 2395. The contents of the literal meaning are holy as a result of their inner meaning: 10126, 10276.

[5] There is also an inner meaning in the historical books of the Word, but it is deep within them: 4989. So just like the prophetic books, the historical books contain hidden treasures of heaven: 755, 1659, 1709, 2310, 2333. Angels take them not as historical information but as doctrinal teachings, because they take them spiritually: 6884. The deep treasures in the historical books are less visible to us than are the ones in the prophetic books because our minds get caught up in focusing on and pondering about historical matters: 2176, 6597. Further discussion of the nature of the inner meaning of the Word (1756, 1984, 2004, 2663, 3035, 7089, 10604, 10614), illustrated with an example (1873).

12   *The Word was composed using correspondences and therefore representa-*
tions. In its literal meaning, the Word was composed entirely by means of
correspondences, that is, by means of things that represent and symbolize
spiritual realities that have to do with heaven and the church: 1404, 1408,
1409, 1540, 1619, 1659, 1709, 1783, 2179, 2763, 2899. This was done so that
there would be an inner meaning in the details (2899); so it was done for
the sake of heaven, because the inhabitants of heaven do not understand
the Word in its literal meaning, which is earthly; they understand it in its
inner meaning, which is spiritual (2899). The Lord spoke using correspondences, representations, and symbolic language because he spoke from his
divine nature: 9049, 9063, 9086, 10126, 10276. This means that the Lord
spoke to the world and at the same time to heaven: 2533, 4807, 9049, 9063,
9086. What the Lord said spread through the whole of heaven: 4637.

The historical events recounted in the Word are representative and
the individual words used are symbolic: 1540, 1659, 1709, 1783, 2686. The
Word could not have been composed in any other style if it was to serve as
a means of communication and connection with the heavens: 2899, 6943,
9481. It is an immense mistake for people to belittle the Word because
of its seemingly simple and inelegant style and to think that they would
accept it if it had been written in a different style: 8783. Indeed, the style
and standard mode of writing among the earliest people in general was
to use correspondences and representative imagery: 605, 1756, 9942. The
early sages enjoyed the Word because of its representative imagery and
symbolism: 2592, 2593 (which include evidence from eyewitness experience). If people of the earliest church had read the Word they would have
seen what is in its inner meaning clearly and what is in its outer meaning
dimly: 4493. Jacob's descendants were led into the land of Canaan because
all the places in that land had been given symbolic meaning from the earliest times (1585, 3686, 4447, 5136, 6516), and so that a Word could be composed there in which places would be mentioned because of their inner
meaning (3686, 4447, 5136, 6516). All the same, the Word was changed in
its outer meaning because of that people, although it was not changed in its
inner meaning: 10453, 10461, 10603, 10604. A collection of passages from
the Word about that people, passages that must, though, be understood in
their inner meaning and not literally: 7051. Since that nation symbolized
the church and since the Word was written in their community and about
them, divine and heavenly things are meant by their names—Reuben, for
example, Simeon, Levi, Judah, Ephraim, Joseph, and the rest; and "Judah"

in its inner sense means the Lord in respect to heavenly love and also his heavenly kingdom: 3654, 3881, 5583, 5782, 6362–6381.

[2] *To show the nature and characteristics of correspondences and of the representative imagery in the Word, I need to say something further about them.* Everything that corresponds to something also represents and therefore means that something, in such a way that the correspondence and the representation unite: 2896, 2899, 2973, 2987, 2989, 2990, 3002, 3225. What correspondence and representation are: 2763, 2987–3002, 3213–3226, 3337–3352, 3472–3485, 4218–4228, 9280 (which include evidence from eyewitness experience and examples). For the early people, the most highly prized body of knowledge was knowledge of correspondences and representative imagery (3021, 3419, 4280, 4748, 4844, 4964, 4966, 6004, 7729, 10252); especially among the people of the Near East (5702, 6692, 7097, 7779, 9391, 10252, 10407); in Egypt more than any other region (5702, 6692, 7097, 7779, 9391, 10407); but also in other nations, such as Greece and elsewhere (2762, 7729). Today, though, it is one of the lost bodies of knowledge, especially in Europe: 2894, 2895, 2995, 3630, 3632, 3747, 3748, 3749, 4581, 4966, 10252. Nevertheless, this body of knowledge truly does transcend all others, since without it we cannot understand the Word, or the meaning of the rituals of the Jewish church that are described in the Word, or what heaven is like, or what spiritual reality is, or how the inflow of what is spiritual into what is earthly happens, or how the inflow of the soul into the body happens, or a great many other matters: 4280, *and the references cited just above.* All the things that are visible to spirits and angels are representative imagery based on correspondences: 1971, 3213–3226, 3475, 3485, 9457, 9481, 9576, 9577. The heavens are full of representative imagery: 1521, 1532, 1619. The deeper you go into the heavens, the more beautiful and perfect are the images that arise: 3475. What these images show you is real because they come from the light of heaven, which is divine truth; and this is the very essential reality from which everything arises: 3485.

[3] The reason absolutely everything that exists in the spiritual world is represented in the earthly world is that the inner reality clothes itself with suitable materials from the outer world as a means of taking on visible form: 6275, 6284, 6299. Just so, a purpose takes on suitable clothing in order to manifest itself as a means in a lower realm and then to manifest itself as something that results on a still lower level; and when a purpose becomes a result through its means it becomes visible, or takes form

before our eyes: 5711. This is illustrated by the inflow of the soul into the body. That is, the soul is clothed with a body that allows those things the soul is thinking and intending to become visible and evident, so when a thought flows down into the body it is represented there by whatever motions and actions correspond to it: 2988. Our minds' emotions are represented so clearly by the various expressions of our faces that they can actually be read there: 4791–4805, 5695. We can see, then, that within absolutely everything in the material world there lie more deeply hidden some means and some purpose from the spiritual world (3562, 5711), because the things that exist in the material world are the final effects into which prior realities are flowing (4240, 4939, 5651, 6275, 6284, 6299, 9216). It is inner realities that are represented and outer ones that do the representing: 4292. (For more on correspondences and representative imagery, see *Heaven and Hell* 87–102, "There Is a Correspondence of Everything in Heaven with Everything in the Human Being"; §§103–115, "There Is a Correspondence of Heaven with Everything Earthly"; and §§170–176, "Representations and Appearances in Heaven.")

[4] Because everything in the material world is symbolic of spiritual and heavenly realities, there were churches in the early times in which all the outer, ritual practices were symbolic. Because of this, these churches were called "symbolic churches": 920, 1361, 2896. The church established among the children of Israel was a symbolic church: 1003, 2179, 10149. All its rituals were outward practices that symbolized inner realities, aspects of heaven and the church: 4288, 4874. The symbolic practices of the church and its worship came to an end when the Lord came into the world and made himself known, since the Lord opened the inner reaches of the church and since, in the highest sense, everything about that church focused on him: 4835.

13 *The literal meaning or outer form of the Word.* The literal meaning of the Word is in keeping with the outward appearance of things in this world (589, 926, 1832, 1874, 2242, 2520, 2533, 2719), and is suited to the comprehension of ordinary people (2533, 9049, 9063, 9086). In its literal meaning, the Word is earthly: 8783. This is because the earthly level is the outermost level to which spiritual and heavenly realities descend and on which they rest, the way a house rests on its foundation; otherwise, the inner meaning without the outer would be like a house without a foundation: 9360, 9430, 9433, 9824, 10044, 10436. Because this is the nature of the Word, it is a vessel that contains spiritual and heavenly meanings (9407); and because this is its nature, there is something holy and divine in absolutely every bit of its literal meaning, right down to the smallest letter (639, 680, 1869, 1870, 9198, 10321, 10637). Even though some laws given for the children of Israel have been annulled, they are still the holy Word because of the inner meaning they contain: 9211, 9259, 9349. Of the laws, judgments, and statutes established for the Israelite or Jewish church (which was a symbolic church), there are some that are still valid in both senses, inner and outer; there are some that are still absolutely mandatory in their literal sense; there are some that can be helpful at our own discretion; and there are some that have been completely annulled: 9349 (which gives details). The Word is divine even in respect to the laws that have been annulled, because there are truths of heaven that lie hidden within their inner meaning: 10637.

What the Word is like in its literal meaning if it is not understood in its inner meaning as well, or what amounts to the same thing, understood according to a true body of teaching drawn from the Word: 10402. A vast number of heresies come into existence from reading the literal meaning without the inner meaning or without a genuine body of teaching drawn from the Word: 10400. People whose interest lies solely in the outer level of the Word apart from what lies within cannot bear the deeper messages of the Word: 10694. That is what the Jews were like, and they still are today: 301, 302, 303, 3479, 4429, 4433, 4680, 4844, 4847, 10396, 10401, 10407, 10694, 10701, 10707.

The Lord is the Word. The sole subject of the deepest meaning of the **14** Word is the Lord, and it describes all the phases of the glorification of his human nature (that is, of its union with the divine nature itself), as well as all the phases of his taking control of the hells and setting in order everything there and in the heavens: 2249, 7014. So in this meaning there is a description of the Lord's whole life in our world, and by means of this there is a constant presence of the Lord with the angels: 2523. At the very center of the Word there is only the Lord, and this is the source of what is divine and holy in the Word: 1873, 9357. The Lord's saying that the Scripture about him was fulfilled [Luke 18:31; 24:44] was referring to everything in the deepest meaning of the Word: 7933.

"The Word" means divine truth: 4692, 5075, 9987. The Lord is the Word because he is divine truth: 2533. The Lord is the Word also because the Word comes from him and is about him (2859); and in its deepest meaning is about no one but the Lord, so the Lord himself is there (1873, 9357); and also because there is a marriage of divine goodness and divine truth throughout the Word and in its every detail, a marriage found only in the Lord (3004, 3005, 3009, 4137, 5194, 5502, 6343, 7945, 8339, 9263, 9314). Divine truth coming from divine goodness is the sole reality, and only what it dwells in—which comes from what is divine—is substantial: 5272, 6880, 7004, 8200. And because divine truth emanating from the Lord as the sun in heaven is heaven's light and divine goodness is its warmth, and because everything there comes into being from that light and warmth the way everything in this world comes into being from earthly light and warmth (which are also present in earthly substances and work through them), and because this earthly world as a whole comes into being by means of heaven or the spiritual world, we can see that everything that has been created has been created from divine truth—that is, from the Word, just as it says in John: "In the beginning was the Word, and the Word was with God, and the Word was God. All things that were made were made through him. *And the Word became flesh*" (John 1:1, 2, 3, 14): 2803, 2894, 5272, 7678. (See *Heaven and Hell* 137 for more on the creation of everything by divine truth and therefore by the Lord; §§116–125 for more about the fact that the sun in heaven is the Lord and that it is his divine love; and §§126–140 on divine truth being light and divine goodness being warmth, both from that sun in heaven.)

A joining together of the Lord and us is accomplished through the Word, by means of its inner meaning: 10375. Absolutely everything in the Word is a means to this joining together, and this is why the Word is more wondrous than anything else that has been written: 10632, 10633, 10634. Now that the Word has been written, the Lord speaks to us through it: 10290. (See also the information presented in *Heaven and Hell* 303–310 about the union of heaven with us by means of the Word.)

15 *People who are hostile to the Word.* People who belittle, blaspheme, and profane the Word: 1878. What they are like in the other life: 1761, 9222. They are like blood disorders: 5719. How dangerous it is to profane the Word: 571, 582. How much harm is done by using the Word to justify premises that are false, especially if they are in support of a love for oneself and for the world: 589. People who do not care about truth for the sake of truth flatly reject whatever has to do with the inner meaning of the Word and are nauseated by it: 5702 (which includes evidence from eyewitness experience of people like this in the world of spirits). About some people in the other life who rejected the deeper contents of the Word; they tried to attack me and went berserk: 1879.

16 *The books that are books of the Word.* The books of the Word are all the Bible books that have an inner meaning. The other Bible books are not the Word. In the Old Testament, the books of the Word are the following: the five books of Moses, the Book of Joshua, the Book of

Judges, the two books of Samuel, the two books of Kings, the Psalms of David, and the prophets—Isaiah, Jeremiah, Lamentations, Ezekiel, Daniel, Hosea, Joel, Amos, Obadiah, Jonah, Micah, Nahum, Habakkuk, Zephaniah, Haggai, Zechariah, and Malachi. In the New Testament: the four Gospels—Matthew, Mark, Luke, and John—and the Book of Revelation. The others do not have an inner meaning: 10325.

The Book of Job is an ancient book in which there is in fact inner meaning, but not in an unbroken chain: 3540, 9942.

More on the Word. In Hebrew, the term "word" has various meanings—speech, a thought of the mind, anything that actually comes into being, and some particular thing: 9987. "The Word" means divine truth and the Lord: 2533, 4692, 5075, 9987. "Words" means truths: 4692, 5075. "Words" also means a whole body of teaching: 1288. The phrase "the Ten Words" means all divine truths: 10688.

Especially in the prophetic books of the Word, there are paired expressions of the same idea, one that refers to goodness and one that refers to truth, which are joined together in this manner: 683, 707, 2173, 8339. The only way to tell which expression refers to goodness and which to truth is from the Word's inner meaning, because there are words that properly express things that are good and words that properly express things that are true: 793, 801. These meanings are so consistent that we can tell just from what the words generally refer to whether that passage has to do with goodness or with truth: 2712. In some instances, too, one expression involves a generalization and the other some particular thing defined by that generalization: 2212. Sometimes in the Word there occurs an alternation in pairs of meanings: 2240 (which includes some discussion). Many things in the Word also have an opposite meaning: 4816. The inner meaning of a statement is in accord with what is being said about the subject: [4502].

In the other life, people who have taken delight in the Word are open to heaven's warmth—which bears heavenly love within itself—in proportion to the nature and extent of their delight in and love for the Word: 1773.

THE END

Biographical Note

Biographical Note

EMANUEL SWEDENBORG (1688–1772) was born Emanuel Swedberg (or Svedberg) in Stockholm, Sweden, on January 29, 1688 (Julian calendar). He was the third of the nine children of Jesper Swedberg (1653–1735) and Sara Behm (1666–1696). At the age of eight he lost his mother. After the death of his only older brother ten days later, he became the oldest living son. In 1697 his father married Sara Bergia (1666–1720), who developed great affection for Emanuel and left him a significant inheritance. His father, a Lutheran clergyman, later became a celebrated and controversial bishop, whose diocese included the Swedish churches in Pennsylvania and in London, England.

After studying at the University of Uppsala (1699–1709), Emanuel journeyed to England, the Netherlands, France, and Germany (1710–1715) to study and work with leading scientists in western Europe. Upon his return he apprenticed as an engineer under the brilliant Swedish inventor Christopher Polhem (1661–1751). He gained favor with Sweden's King Charles XII (1682–1718), who gave him a salaried position as an overseer of Sweden's mining industry (1716–1747). Although Emanuel was engaged, he never married.

After the death of Charles XII, Emanuel was ennobled by Queen Ulrika Eleonora (1688–1741), and his last name was changed to Swedenborg (or Svedenborg). This change in status gave him a seat in the Swedish House of Nobles, where he remained an active participant in the Swedish government throughout his life.

A member of the Royal Swedish Academy of Sciences, he devoted himself to studies that culminated in a number of publications, most notably a comprehensive three-volume work on natural philosophy and metallurgy (1734) that brought him recognition across Europe as a scientist. After 1734 he redirected his research and publishing to a study of anatomy in search of the interface between the soul and body, making several significant discoveries in physiology.

From 1743 to 1745 he entered a transitional phase that resulted in a shift of his main focus from science to theology. Throughout the rest of his life he maintained that this shift was brought about by Jesus Christ, who appeared to him, called him to a new mission, and opened his perception to a permanent dual consciousness of this life and the life after death.

He devoted the last decades of his life to studying Scripture and publishing eighteen theological titles that draw on the Bible, reasoning, and his own spiritual experiences. These works present a Christian theology with unique perspectives on the nature of God, the spiritual world, the Bible, the human mind, and the path to salvation.

Swedenborg died in London on March 29, 1772 (Gregorian calendar), at the age of eighty-four.